San Diego

CW01590422

Discovery CHANNEL

APA PUBLICATIONS
Part of the Langenscheidt Publishing Group

Eugene
Springfield
Bend
Portland
Boise
Arco
Caldwell
Brothers
Riley
Burns
Harney Basin
Coos Bay
Roseburg
Mt Thielsen 9182
Chemult
CRATER LAKE NP
Oregon
Jordan Valley
Shoshone
Idaho
Paisley
Twin Falls
Grants Pass
Upper Klamath Lake
Valley Falls
Drake Peak 8406
Owyhee
Medford
Klamath Falls
New Pine Creek
Goose Lake
McDermitt
Matterhorn 10840
Crescent City
LAVA BEDS NM
Duffer Peak 9396
Kings
Granite Peak 9731
REDWOOD NP
Klamath
Klamath Mts
Mt Shasta 14163
Alturas
Eagle Peak 9892
Wells
Salt Lake City
Cascade Range
Clair Engle Lake
Winnemucca
Humboldt
Elko
Wendover
WHISKEYTOWN-SHASTA-TRINITY NRA
Ruby Dome 11388
Eureka
Redding
Lassen Peak 10457
LASSEN VOLCANIC NP
Susanville
Mt Tobin 9774
Coast Ranges
Red Bluff
Pyramid Lake
Nevada
Eel
Cummings
Chico
Reno
Sparks
Fallon
Austin
Ely
Sacramento
Yuba City
Ukiah
Carson City
Lake Tahoe
Shoshone Mts
Reese
Currant Mtn 11512
Wheeler Pk 13063
Mt Jefferson 11949
GREAT BASIN
GREAT BASIN NP
Point Arena
SIERRA NEVADA
Santa Rosa
Napa
Hawthorne
Warm Springs
POINT REYES NS
Point Reyes
Stockton
YOSEMITE NP
Mono Lake
Tonopah
Caliente
Boundary Peak 13140
San Francisco
Oakland
Modesto
Merced
San Joaquin
Bishop
Las Vegas
San Jose
Los Banos
Santa Cruz
KINGS CANYON NP
Beatty
Salinas
Fresno
Mt Whitney 14495
DEATH VALLEY NP
White
Monterey
PINNACLES NM
Visalia
SEQUOIA NP
Telescope Peak 11049
Lake Mead
Point Sur
Kern
Henderson
LAKE MEAD NRA
Boulder City
PACIFIC OCEAN
California
Paso Robles
Ridgecrest
Bullhead City
Mojave Desert
Kingman
San Luis Obispo
Bakersfield
MOJAVE N PRES
Barstow
Santa Maria
Needles
Lancaster
Point Arguello
Santa Barbara
Ventura
Pasadena
San Bernardino
Colorado
Phoenix
Santa Barbara Channel
Oxnard
Riverside
San Miguel
Santa Cruz
Anacapa
JOSHUA TREE NP
CHANNEL ISLANDS NP
Santa Rosa
Los Angeles
Palm Springs
Blythe
Anaheim
Santa Barbara
Santa Catalina
Salton Sea
San Nicolas
Oceanside
Escondido
Tucson
Channel Islands
San Clemente
San Diego
Yuma
Mexicali
Tijuana
San Luis Río Colorado
Rosarito
MEXICO
Ensenada
California
100 miles / 160 km

Welcome

This guidebook combines the interests and enthusiasms of two of the world's best-known information providers: Insight Guides, who have set the standard for visual travel guides since 1970, and Discovery Channel, the world's premier source of non-fiction television programming. Its aim is to bring you the best of the San Diego area in a series of tailor-made itineraries devised by Insight's correspondent in California, John Wilcock.

San Diego is the oldest city on the West Coast and one of the nation's most fascinating. Traces of its long history – from its discovery by Juan Rodriguez Cabrillo, through years of Spanish rule, economic booms, and California's incorporation into the USA – color the whole city. Today the historic Old Town testifies to a rich past of heroes and villains, a modern center is a hub of commerce and entertainment, and luxurious beachside suburbs exemplify fine living. This book captures the city and its environs in a series of walking and driving itineraries and includes excursions to exciting destinations not far from the city – to the desert, vineyards, a former gold-mining town, and south of the border to Mexico. There are sections on shopping, eating out and nightlife, plus a calendar of special events and a fact-packed chapter of information including a list of hand-picked hotels.

John Wilcock has always liked San Diego, not least because he has an affinity with all places big enough to offer variety but small enough to walk around. Downtown San Diego fulfils those criteria, and all of the city's other interesting parts, such as Old Town, Sea World, and Coronado, can be easily reached (after parking the car) by the ubiquitous Old Town trolley. The city enjoys a fabulous climate that surpasses even that of Los Angeles – its big-city neighbor to the north.

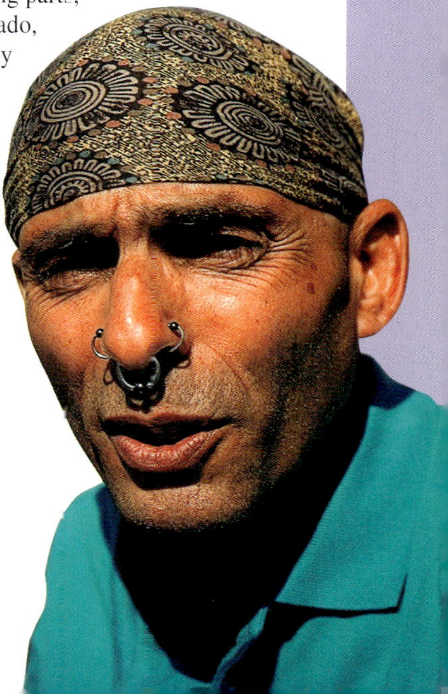

contents

HISTORY AND CULTURE

CITY ITINERARIES

The first eight tours explore San Diego's essential sights, from the downtown waterfront area and 'Old Town', site of the original Spanish mission, to the beaches of salubrious Coronado, a short hop across the bay. They incorporate cutting-edge museums, historic buildings and artifacts, San Diego's world-famous zoo and the affluent suburbs of La Jolla and Del Mar.

Excursions

Seven excursions to destinations within easy reach.

Leisure Activities

Calendar of Events

Practical Information

Maps

Index and Credits

Pages 2/3: aboard the Coronado ferry
Pages 8/9: monumental tribute at the Sports Museum

23

History & Culture

San Diego, once the home of the Ipai and Tapai Indians – of whom few traces remain – is the birthplace of white civilization on the West Coast, hence the appellation 'the Plymouth of the West.' It is the oldest city in California and, after Los Angeles, the biggest. It was the first city in the region to cultivate fields, build an irrigation system, and establish a school.

Only 50 years after Columbus discovered America, navigator Juan Rodriguez Cabrillo was sent north from the coast of New Spain (Mexico) to find 'a landlocked and very good harbor.' He arrived on September 8, 1542, the feast day of the Franciscan San Diego de Alcala, whose name Cabrillo took for the site. Sixty years passed before the arrival of a second Spanish captain, Sebastian Vizcaino, who declared the area 'a fine place for Spanish settlement.' Fine it might have been, but it was ignored until late in the following century when Spain became worried that Russia or England might move south from their northern California outposts and claim the territory. Thus land and sea expeditions set off from Baja.

'The whole land expedition arrived without having lost a single man' Father Crespi confided in his diary, 'although they were on half rations and with no more provisions than three sacks of flour, of which each man received two cakes for his entire day's ration.'

Meeting the Indians

Father Junipero Serra arrived with another party, also without incident, except for his shock at meeting a group of Indians who 'were entirely naked, as Adam in the garden, before sin.' Serra was impressed by San Diego, which he found to be beautiful and also blessed with acorns, wild asparagus and grapes. 'There are so many vines grown by nature and without human help,' he noted, 'that it would mean little expense to follow the example of our good father Noe [Noah]… In short it is a good country – distinctly better than Old California.' He rejoiced at 'a harvest of souls that might readily be gathered into the bosom of our Holy Mother, the Church, and it would appear, with very little trouble.'

The seafaring expedition was less fortunate: all but two of the sailors on the *San Carlos* died en route, as did more than a third of those aboard the *San Antonio*. Nevertheless, all the new arrivals gathered on July 16, 1769 to celebrate at Presidio Hill, which, shortly afterwards, Serra chose as the site of the West Coast's first mission. By the dawn of the 19th century, Presidio Hill's population had reached 167.

In 1822 the long-festering Mexican rebellion against Spain finally brought Spanish rule to an end. A newly

Left: the traditions of local tribal life were destroyed by the missions. **Right:** Cabrillo National Monument

independent Mexico took over San Diego, established its own *pueblo* (village of Pueblo peoples) and closed the mission, which had moved 5 miles (8km) to the east. The writer Richard Henry Dana Jr described the *pueblo* as 'about 40 dark brown looking huts... and three or four larger ones, white-washed, which belong to the *gente de razón* [upper class].'

In 1846, the year that the explorer John C Fremont raised the US flag, Don Pedro C Carillo, son of San Diego's collector of customs, had his request for a grant of 4,185 acres (1,700ha) of brush and sand dunes across the bay accepted. After three frustrating years of attempts to raise cattle on the barren acres, Don Pedro sold the Peninsula de San Diego Rancho. Although the area's ranches played their part in curing hides for the trading ships that plied the coast, they didn't share the prosperity of their northern counterparts. Some 35 years later the peninsula was acquired by an Indiana railroad tycoon, Elisha S Babcock, and turned into Coronado.

In 1850, when San Diego consisted of the Old Town centered around the Presidio, William Heath Davis built a wharf at the foot of what is now Market Street and tried to found a new community. (Davis, a San Francisco merchant who had married into San Diego's Estudillo family, first arrived on American shores aged nine. He traveled on the same ship as French-born Jean-Louis Vignes, later to become California's first professional winemaker. Vignes told the young Davis that he had written home to France predicting that some day California would be its equal in producing wine; as an adult, Davis acquired grape vines from Europe and eventually came to own the largest vineyard in the state.) Unfortunately a fire destroyed his property in San Francisco, and he abandoned his fledgling community on San Diego's waterfront. The buildings were moved back to the Old Town.

The Arrival of Alonzo Horton

By the time Alonzo Horton, then aged 54, arrived on April 15, 1867, from northern California, the coastal site had been long deserted. But Horton, who had made $5,000 selling ice from the El Dorado Mountains, saw its potential and paid the county clerk to auction the land. With the memory of Davis's failure still fresh, it was not only Old Town residents who were skeptical. When Capt. Phineas Banning, who operated a San Pedro tugboat, heard that a friend was headed for San Diego, he offered him 50 cents, saying: 'Here, take this and buy Horton's Addition for me. You can keep the change.'

Horton was undeterred. He had already founded Hortonville, a small community 20 miles (32km) from Oshkosh in Wisconsin. Now in San Diego he bought 900 acres (365ha), built a wharf and opened up Main Street (today's

Above: Mexican rule did not last long. **Above Right:** plaque in Old Town State Historic Park
Right: the completion of the coast-to-coast railroad contributed to the economic boom

5th Street) by offering free lots on condition that buyers would build their homes along it near the waterfront. He moved into the two-story frame house he had built for himself at 6th & A streets in 1873. Davis's old house became the New Town's first hotel and soon more people were arriving than could be accommodated in it. The newcomers bought lots and camped on them while building homes. One offered Horton $250,000 for his new town. Horton declined to sell.

A second hotel, The Bayview, went up at 5th and F streets, advertising that 'the climate of San Diego is the most delightful and health-giving on the Pacific Slope. Persons seeking health and recreation can find no pleasanter place in the Golden State.' The hotel was demolished in 1889 and replaced with The Palms. By this time even some of Old Town's residents were starting to relocate to the new site, and their weekly newspaper, the *San Diego Union*, was at loggerheads with the new town's *San Diego Bulletin*.

Jealousy in Los Angeles

The arrival of the transcontinental railroad in 1885 sparked a real estate boom and caused intense jealousy in Los Angeles, which did everything it could to discourage its citizens from visiting its southern neighbor. Rail passengers bound for San Diego were intercepted and persuaded that their destination was just a sleepy Mexican town with unpaved streets and no water. Some naive visitors were still clutching the jugs of water they had been sold as they disembarked in the southern city. Horton was by now in his seventies and his influence was waning, but his vision had been confirmed. Today his name lives on in Horton Plaza, which in his lifetime was just an undeveloped piece of land in the city center. 'He was a plain, typical American western pioneer, with a true vision and optimism infinite,' according to John B Osborne's eulogy at Horton's funeral in 1909.

Another such pioneer was John D Spreckels, heir to a San Francisco

family that made a fortune from Hawaiian sugar. In 1887, when the land rush was at its peak – it was to collapse the following year with several bank failures – Spreckels was cruising off the southern California coast in his luxury yacht, the *Lurline*. On finding that the icebox door had been left open and the food spoilt, he set ashore at the new port of San Diego to replenish his supplies. He liked what he saw and, while ashore, he happened to meet Elisha S Babcock, a piano manufacturer from Chicago.

Together with Hampton L Story, Babcock had paid $110,000 for what had been the Peninsula de San Diego Rancho and, as president of the Coronado Beach Company, he established a railroad. It ran from downtown all the way round the peninsula to what he planned to be the world's biggest seaside hotel, the Hotel del Coronado. For architects, Babcock and Story hired the inexperienced Reid brothers from Illinois; for lumber they commissioned a San Francisco redwood mill's entire output. The mill was also the source of several hundred of their Chinese laborers. An impressed Spreckels bought into the company, and within five years – after Babcock suffered heavily in the 1888 financial crash – he and his brother Adolph were sole owners.

After water-supply problems had been solved – wells were dug near Old Town and the water piped across the bay – the Hotel Del, as it was dubbed, opened in 1888, its 399 rooms starting at $3 a night. For modern, efficient coal-handling facilities, Spreckels built a $90,000 wharf at the foot of G Street to service the Santa Fe Railroad, even allowing its rival, the ailing California Southern Railroad, to take coal on credit. He acquired the *San Diego Union* in 1890, the *Evening Tribune* in 1901 and, with Babcock, organized a firm to bring water from the mountains 60 miles (96km) away to the new Morena Dam.

Tent City

Once he had established a chain of transportation facilities around the region, and developed Mission Beach, Spreckels turned his attention back to Coronado, creating Tent City on the strand below the grand hotel. Rows of tent cottages with bare floors, palm thatch roofs and simple furniture plus a washstand and pitcher, served as a weekend vacation spot for hundreds of San Diegans. They thronged to the recreation center and restaurant, and danced to live music from the bandshell. A former ferry, the 528-ton steam-powered *Silver Gate*, was moored offshore and turned into a casino. After the 1906 San Francisco earthquake, Spreckels moved to San Diego, where he built a big home opposite the Hotel Del.

In the 1890s, E W Scripps moved to California, where he loaned two young newspapermen $3,000 to buy the relatively insignificant *San Diego Sun*. The pair spent $18,000 of his money with little success, whereupon he turned the title over to another fledgling publisher, W H Porterfield, who put the paper on a solid financial footing. It was the beginning of Scripps's media empire, which eventually comprised a score of dailies, 10 television stations, five radio stations and the world's largest features syndicate.

'It was the nation's first popular press,' accord-

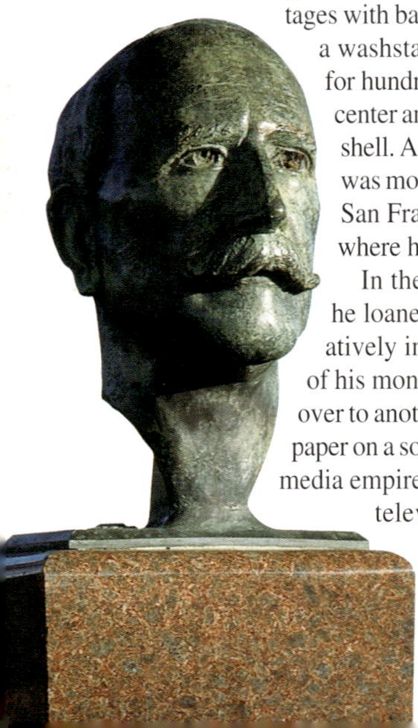

Left: John D Spreckels

ing to one Jack Casserly, 'low on cost, high on sensationalism and soaring into mass circulation. The Scrippses practiced Yellow Journalism long before William Randolph Hearst and Joseph Pulitzer made it a household phrase.' For all his success in tabloid journalism, Scripps's lasting legacy to San Diego was the Scripps Institute of Biological Research (now known as the Scripps Institute for Oceanographic Research), which he founded with the intention of developing a school of scientists free of all dogma.

When the Panama Canal was completed in 1914, San Diego chose to copy one of San Francisco's ideas and hold a celebratory exposition. As the southernmost US city on the coast, it could be reached by northbound vessels long before its Bay City rival. San Diegans agreed to spare no expense on the Panama-California International Exposition of 1915. Originally it seemed that a local architect, Irving Gill, would be chosen to create the buildings proposed for Balboa Park. Gill, who had arrived in San Diego from Chicago in 1893, was already responsible for the Scripps Institute of Oceanography, the Holly Sefton Memorial Hospital for Children and the five-story Wilson Acton Hotel in La Jolla. Fond of concrete's qualities of plasticity and durability, Gill experimented with concrete monolithic construction and was widely admired for his forthrightness and honesty.

'Unparalleled in the History of the World'

'The West,' Gill declared in the portentous tones of a visionary, 'has an opportunity unparalleled in the history of the world, for it is the newest white page turned for registration. In California we have the great, wide plains, arched blue skies that are fresh chapters as yet unwritten.' Expressing his architectural philosophy in *The Craftsman* in May 1916 he wrote: 'There is something very restful and satisfying to my mind in the simple cube house with creamy walls, sheer and plain, rising boldly into the sky, unrelieved by cornices or overhang of roof... I like the bare honesty of these houses, the childlike frankness and chaste simplicity of them.'

Above: lily pond and Casa del Prado, Balboa Park

For an international exposition that, it was hoped, would truly place the city on the map, however, San Diego's planners sought something more sophisticated. So, for all his pragmatic philosophy, and many admirers, Gill was overlooked and the position awarded to Bertram Goodhue, an expert on Spanish colonial architecture. And indeed the exposition spread San Diego's reputation as a place for good living that offered mild, year-around temperatures suitable for growing out-of-season vegetables and fruits, along with a cost-of-living some three percent less than that of comparable cities.

A Military Center

For all the undoubted success of the exposition, the real reason for San Diego's lasting significance was the arrival of the US military early in the 20th century, at first for training purposes, and then with the establishment of army, naval and aircraft bases. By the 1930s, the military payroll for such institutions as the North Island Naval Air Station on Coronado and the Miramar Naval Air Station to the north topped $2 million per month.

In 1927 the North Island station served as the take-off point for Charles Lindbergh's famous transatlantic flight aboard the *Spirit of St Louis*. It took only 60 days to construct the airplane on the site of what is now a solar engineering plant south of the San Diego airport. Lindbergh had prepared for the ordeal by practicing sleep derivation in his car in the parking lot. Aircraft production and defense contracts brought considerable prosperity and mass employment to San Diego in the middle years of the 20th century.

In recent years, a renaissance of the once industrial downtown harbor area has seen the emergence of the kind of soaring, enlivening architecture that befits California's second-largest city. In the impressive Civic Center, a bronze plaque that pays tribute to the city's founder, Alonzo Horton (1813–1909) bears the legend: 'First in civic vision, first in heroic adventure, first in courage and determination. Here he founded the city of his dreams.'

Above: Charles Lindbergh and the plane in which he made the first solo Atlantic crossing

History Highlights

1542 Juan Rodriguez Cabrillo arrives at San Diego, which he names and claims for Spain.

1602 Sebastian Vizcaino proclaims the site 'a fine place for a harbor'

1769 Father Junipero Serra builds the first of a chain of 21 missions.

1774 Mission San Diego de Alcala relocates 6 miles (9km) inland along the San Diego River.

1775 Indians surround Mission San Diego de Alcala, set fire to its fragile wooden structures and attack a small contingent of Spaniards. The survivors withdraw to the Presidio.

1784 Father Junipero Serra, aged 70, dies at Monterey.

1795 Manuel de Vargas opens the first public school.

1798 Founding of Mission San Luis Rey which, until the mid-1800s, is the largest structure in California.

1812 Earthquake destroys the San Diego Mission church, which is rebuilt in 1813.

1822 The Mexican flag is raised over the Presidio after revolutionaries bring an end to Spanish rule. California pledges allegiance to Mexico.

1826 Jedediah Smith, the first American to arrive overland in San Diego, opens a route from Salt Lake City.

1848 The Mexican-American War ends; San Diego becomes an American possession.

1850 California achieves statehood; San Diego becomes its first county. William Heath Davis builds a wharf in the harbor and attempts unsuccessfully to found a new town.

1867 Alonzo Horton creates a new city beside San Diego Bay.

1868 The city is the first west of the Mississippi to designate land for an urban public park.

1870 Gold is discovered in the East County mountain town of Julian.

1872 Fire destroys most of Old Town.

1887 San Diego's Electric Rapid Transit Company inaugurates the first electric street railroad system in the western United States.

1888 John D Spreckels becomes sole owner of the new Hotel del Coronado.

1904 The Hotel del Coronado, the largest wooden structure in the US, introduces the world's first electrically lit Christmas tree.

1909 City founder and local legend Alonzo Horton dies.

1912 In a wave of civic morality, police clean up the Gaslamp Quarter and arrest 112 prostitutes.

1915 Balboa Park hosts the Panama-California Exposition.

1923 First nonstop coast-to-coast flight (2,780 miles/4,474km) from New York to San Diego's North Island takes 26 hrs 50 minutes.

1927 Charles Lindbergh completes the first transatlantic flight to Paris in the San Diego-built *Spirit of St Louis*.

1947 First transcontinental helicopter flight lands at North Island.

1970 Opening of San Diego-La Jolla Underwater Park, the West Coast's first.

1973 The world's first Omnimax (now IMAX) theater opens in Balboa Park.

1990 Hatching of the first emperor penguin chick outside of Antarctica takes place at SeaWorld.

1988 Hotel del Coronado celebrates its centenary.

1998 Almost 20,000 runners participate in the Suzuki Rock'n'Roll Marathon, the world's largest first-time marathon race.

1998 First breeding in captivity of a pair of California condors in the San Diego Wild Animal Park.

2000 *Men's Fitness* magazine proclaims San Diego to be 'America's fittest city'.

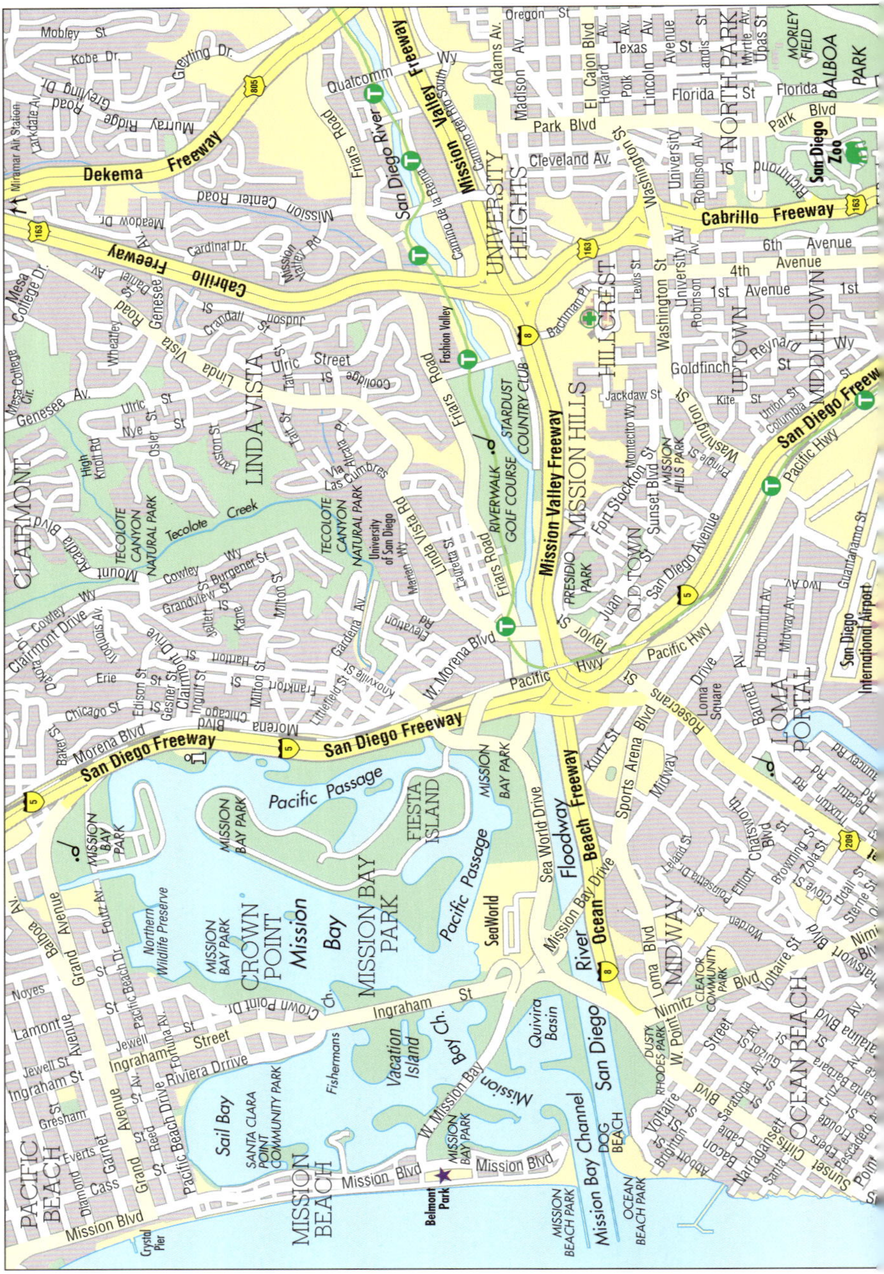
CLAIRMONT
LINDA VISTA
UNIVERSITY HEIGHTS
HILLCREST
MISSION HILLS
OLD TOWN
UPTOWN
MIDDLETOWN
NORTH PARK
BALBOA PARK
San Diego Zoo
MORLEY FIELD
LOMA PORTAL
MIDWAY
OCEAN BEACH
PACIFIC BEACH
MISSION BEACH
CROWN POINT
MISSION BAY PARK
Mission Bay
FIESTA ISLAND
Pacific Passage
SeaWorld
Vacation Island
Fishermans Ch.
Bay Ch.
Quivira Basin
Sail Bay
SANTA CLARA POINT COMMUNITY PARK
Northern Wildlife Preserve
Belmont Park
Crystal Pier
DOG BEACH
OCEAN BEACH PARK
MISSION BEACH PARK
Mission Bay Channel
San Diego River Floodway
San Diego International Airport
TECOLOTE CANYON NATURAL PARK
Tecolote Creek
University of San Diego
PRESIDIO PARK
MISSION HILLS PARK
RIVERWALK GOLF COURSE
STARDUST COUNTRY CLUB
Fashion Valley
CLEATOR COMMUNITY PARK
DUSTY RHODES PARK
San Diego Freeway
Mission Valley Freeway
Cabrillo Freeway
Dekema Freeway
Ocean Beach Freeway
Mission Valley
Pacific Hwy
Morena Blvd
Linda Vista Road
Friars Road
Mission Blvd
Ingraham Street
Sports Arena Blvd
Rosecrans St
Nimitz Blvd
Sunset Cliffs Blvd
Washington St
University Av.
Park Blvd
El Cajon Blvd
Miramar Air Station

San Diego
1500 yards / 1600 m
San Diego Bay
PACIFIC OCEAN
CORONADO
North Island Naval Air Station
POINT LOMA
Point Loma
PENINSULA
LA PLAYA
CENTRE CITY
SHERMAN HEIGHTS
BARRIO LOGAN
Shelter Island
Harbor Island
HARBOR ISLAND DRIVE PARK
SHORELINE PARK BEACH
PACIFIC RIM PARK
America's Cup Harbor
Shelter Island Yacht Basin
U.S. Coast Guard Station
Maritime Museum
Santa Fe Depot (Union Station)
Museum of Contemporary Art
Seaport Village
San Diego Convention Center
EMBARCADERO MARINA PARK
Horton Plaza
Ferry Landing Marketplace
San Diego-Coronado Ferry
TIDELANDS PARK
CROSBY ST PARK
Coronado Toll Bridge
CORONADO GOLF COURSE
GLORIETTA BAY PARK
Glorietta Bay
Hotel del Coronado
SEA 'N AIR GOLF COURSE
SUNSET PARK
U.S. Naval Amphibious Base
Silver Strand Boulevard
Silver Strand State Beach, Imperial Beach
28th Street Pier
Zuniga Pt
Ballast Pt
Cabrillo National Monument
Monument Headquarters
Old Point Loma Lighthouse
Operational Lighthouse
Cabrillo Memorial Drive
Fort Rosecrans Military Reservation
FORT ROSECRANS NATIONAL CEMETERY
U.S. Naval Reservation
Catalina Blvd
Canon Street
Rosecrans
SUNSET CLIFFS PARK
Ratkay Pt
NEWBREAK BEACH
Rock Pile
Ocean Boulevard
Orange Avenue
San Diego Freeway
Harbor Drive
Pacific Hwy

nal to the **America's Cup Museum** (daily 10am–6pm; tel: 619-685-1413) whose exhibits tell the story of sailing's most prestigious award. The annual race for America's Schooner Cup takes place every March in the waters between Harbor Island and the tip of Point Loma. Harbor excursions and the Coronado Ferry leave from the piers where Broadway meets the sea, and in season there are whale-watching cruises, some of which head down as far south as Baja.

12 Theme Cafés

Beyond the piers is the attractively designed **Seaport Village** (tel: 619-235-4014), a 14-acre (5.5-ha) complex of restaurants (one of which is literally over the water) and stores of all kinds. This is the place to get flags and such whimsical items as music boxes and magic tricks. Check out the San Diego City Store for local memorabilia. Eateries along the paved walkways beside the water include a dozen theme cafés. There are some 70 stores, a video arcade, a century-old carousel and a chiming Victorian clock tower.

Next to the clock tower, the **Embarcadero Marine Park** attracts artists, clowns, kite flyers, and picnickers. Across the trolley route from the soaring Convention Center, the **Children's Museum** (Tues–Fri 10am–3pm, weekends 10am–4pm; tel: 619-233-KIDS) has a supervised play area in which children are encouraged to create artworks with paints or clay. The

museum park, which runs parallel to Harbor Drive, has a children's playground. Check out Dr Martin Luther King Jr Promenade, along which the pavement is etched with quotes from the esteemed civil rights leader.

Not far away (stop No. 4 on the trolley) the amazing Marriott Hotel, its two shiny wings resembling a ship in full sail, is located on a marina. There's some sensational architecture down here: the 40-story Hyatt for example – the tallest waterfront hotel in the country – rises to twice the height of the arched Coronado Bridge. The new structures currently rising all around are revitalizing an area once filled with tuna canning factories.

Heading back up through town, pass the yellow-frame **William Heath Davis House** (Mon–Fri 10am–2pm, Sat 10am–1pm; tel: 619-233-5227) at Island and 4th streets. This was the mid-19th century home of the San Diego pioneer whose attempt to build a new city here had to be abandoned. The prefabricated 'salt box' house was shipped from the East Coast in 1850. Until acquired by the city in 1981 it still used gaslight fittings.

You are now on the edge of the **Gaslamp Quarter**, the 16-block, once rowdy area of boisterous saloons to which every sailor headed as soon as his ship hit port. In the latter half of the century, when gas lamps illuminated the wooden sidewalks, ships' chandlers outfitted tall, masted clippers here on the boats' last stop before heading for Cape Horn. The Chinese merchant Aw Quin opened an office in the quarter to broker deals involving Chinese labor needed to construct the California Southern Railway. Who knows how many amorous adventurers bought the Chinese love potions made from rhinoceros horn that were sold here.

The Notorious Wyatt Earp

Wyatt Earp, described by Yale's John Mack Faragher as 'a frontier demimonde – sometime lawman but fulltime gambler, confidence man, associate of pimps and prostitutes,' ran a couple of saloons on the sites of today's Palace Pawnbrokers on 4th Street and Rogers Restaurant on 5th. According to the historian, Earp 'kept company with the saloon crowd and quickly developed a reputation as a bad case'. When Earp was himself asked later in life about his occupation, he replied: 'Well, I dealt awhile in pasteboard and ivory.'

Earp bought and sold property, owned racehorses and refereed boxing bouts, bullfights and, across the Mexican border, cockfights. His wife Josephine said horses were 'the love of his life', and at the San Diego racetrack he would meet up with another famous gambler, 'Lucky' Baldwin, in the days when the

Above Left: Seaport Village
Right: gas lamp, William Heath Davis House

city 'combined the climate of Hawaii with the licentiousness of the Barbary Coast', in the words of Allen Barra.

Earp came to San Diego in the late 1880s (some years after the legendary encounter at the OK Corral in Tombstone, Arizona), whereupon he was listed in the city directory as a 'capitalist' living on the Schmitt block. His first apartment adjoined the Wells Fargo office. In addition to his saloons he set up gambling joints at 6th near the Hotel James, on E near 6th, and on 4th between D & E across the Plaza. Men would ride for miles in the hope of winning a fortune at the blackjack, poker, or faro tables.

Gambling halls and prostitution were rampant until 1912 when the police moved in to arrest the hookers and close down the whole Red Light district. Today horse-drawn carriages circulate through the old streets past Victorian buildings occupied by businesses, fashionable restaurants, art galleries, and specialty stores. The **Historical Foundation** (tel: 619-233-4692) organizes Saturday morning walking tours starting from the William Heath Davis House.

On 4th Avenue, between Island Avenue and Market Street, you will find the popular community arts Hahn Cosmopolitan Theatre on the site of a 1920s dance hall. This is the **Asian/Pacific Thematic Historic District**, where 20 historic Asian structures were built between 1883 and 1930. At 3rd & Island is the **Horton Grand Hotel**, which was moved from an unknown location and restored to its full Victorian splendor. Orientalists will love the **Chinese Historical Museum** (Tues–Sat 10.30am–4pm, Sun noon–4pm; tel: 619-338-9888). It dates from 1927 and tells the story of this remarkable neighborhood.

The City's First Skyscraper

On E Street, a 1913 marble affair known as **Gaslamp Plaza Suites** was originally the Watts-Robinson Building, the city's first skyscraper. Half a block farther south on 5th Avenue is the even older (1888) **Louis Bank of Commerce**, the city's first granite building on whose first floor an oyster bar (long gone) was one of Wyatt Earp's hangouts. On the next corner is the 1890 Romanesque Revival-style **Keating Bulding**. A museum devoted to Earp can be found in Market Street's Gaslamp Books.

Horton Plaza is a curvilinear early project with Jon Jerde's Escher-like walkways. Jerde, who believes that architecture's prime task is to create public spaces in which

Above: the Louis Bank of Commerce building dates to 1888
Right: even after the advent of electricity, the name remains

people can experience 'a sense of common identity', later designed Los Angeles's Universal City Walk. Horton Plaza has been much admired for its imaginative style and vibrant color scheme. The five brightly colored floors of ramps, stairs, escalators, elevators, and decorative pillars seem to flow into each other. Anchored by such stalwarts as Abercrombie & Fitch, Eddie Bauer, and Williams-Sonoma, it contains a food court and is open from 10am until 9pm on weekdays, until 6 or 7pm on weekends. The $140 million. mall was named after Alonzo Horton, who in 1867 bought 960 acres (390ha) of waterfront land for $265, built a pier and sold residential lots.

Horton built Horton's Hall at 6th & F streets as a venue for concerts, drama and meetings. He started a steamship line to rival the existing one as a way to reduce the exorbitant fares that he felt were inhibiting the town's growth. And he offered brushes and lime to householders to whitewash their homes. When owners were recalcitrant, he hired workers to do the job; with the overall aesthetic of the city in mind, he would decide which houses, or which of their sides, needed the painters' attention.

For years he kept the land at Broadway between 3rd and 4th streets as a recreational open space, Horton's Plaza, but he sold it to the city in his declining years. At the age of 95, just before his death in 1909, he lost his properties to taxes and foreclosure but proclaimed: 'It's [still] the most beautiful place in the world to me and I would rather have the affection of friendly greetings of San Diegans than all the rulers in the world.'

English Afternoon Tea

The last trolley leaves Horton Plaza for Coronado at 4.40pm (5.40 in summer). If there's time you might want to walk one block up to Broadway for some relaxation in the sumptuous lounge of the U S Grant Hotel, where you can listen to the Pianola (unmanned piano). Help yourself to a rosy Washington apple from the bowl on the reception desk and admire the opulent chandeliers. Or you may want to settle down for a typically English afternoon tea, served

Above: the Horton Plaza shopping center is admired for its imaginative style

on delicate porcelain from a teapot wearing a flowered woolen cosy. At $14 it's not a bargain, but you get finger sandwiches, a crumpet, a scone with Devon cream and miniature pastries. Alternatively you could walk along Broadway to Kettner Street's **Museum of Contemporary Art** (Tues–Sat 10am–5pm, Sun noon–5pm; tel: 858-454-3541), an annex to the museum in La Jolla. (*see page 42*). Along C Street, the trolley route a block north, the city's first department store went up between 5th and 6th streets. At the time it was so far uptown that for years it was called Marston's Folly.

The magnificent **Union Station** at Broadway and Kettner Street is a stop for AMTRAK trains. The station (1915) was built in Spanish Colonial Revival style with redwood beam ceilings and tiled walls by San Francisco architects Bakewell and Brown when San Diego hoped to be the western terminus of the Continental Railroad. At the grand opening prior to the Panama-California International Exposition, the first ticket buyer was Oliver Stough, the last veteran of the Mexican War.

A Queen Anne-style House

On the edge of town, east of the I-5 freeway, the elegant **Villa Montezuma** (Fri–Sun 10am–4pm; tel: 619-299-2211) at 20th and K streets, was built for the concert pianist, singer and spiritualist Benjamin Sheppard, who was 38 when he arrived in San Diego in 1887. He was so popular that his fans raised the money for his extravagant home. Sheppard's flamboyant taste can be deduced from the Queen Anne-style house with its onion dome. Stained glass windows feature portraits of Beethoven, Mozart, Raphael, Goethe, Shakespeare, and others; the interiors are furnished with redwood paneling, heavy Persian rugs and ebony panels inlaid with ivory.

Above: Santa Fe depot
Left: the museum flies the flags

2. CORONADO *(see map, p28)*

This leisurely day in Coronado, a short hop across the bay, makes a pleasant change from the busy downtown area .

The SR75 highway to Coronado crosses the bay over a toll bridge high enough for aircraft carriers to pass beneath. The first person to drive across the bridge was the then Secretary of the Navy, Franklin D Roosevelt, in 1915. The longer route via south San Diego – along which an electric tram used to run – is now covered by the 901 bus every half hour until midnight. The most pleasant journey is on the Bay Ferry that leaves San Diego's B Street Pier every hour on the hour. The trip to Ferry Landing Marketplace (tel: 619-435-8895), which has stores, a fishing pier, and a sandy beach, costs $2 and takes 15 minutes. Water taxis (tel: 619-235-8294) are also available.

Coronado, where the average price of a house is $600,000 and the golf club charges a $20 green fee, looks its best when lit up at night. But if you're tired after visiting the downtown area you might want to explore it by day and stay over for dinner. At the southern end, **Imperial Beach** (pop: 23,000) is a series of sandy strands that stretches from Coronado all the way down to the Tijuana bullring. The area is increasingly being settled by the wealthy denizens of Los Angeles and Orange counties.

Sand Castles and Seaplanes

Every July, Imperial Beach hosts the US Open Sand Castle Competition. Farther north, where the peninsula narrows, **Silver Strand State Beach** offers calm waters and a picnic area complete with overnight camping for RVs (recreational vehicles). A century ago families flocked here for inexpensive vacations in Tent City, where live entertainment and a relaxed, communal atmosphere more than compensated for the primitive accommodations. The Naval Air Station at the northern end of Coronado played a significant part in aviation history – it was the site of the world's first successful seaplane flight (1911); the first night flight (1913); the first mid-air refueling between two planes (1923); and, in the same year, the nation's first transcontinental flight.

Almost everything in the town of Coronado, including Spreckels Park, where a band plays on summer Sundays, is on or close to Orange Avenue. Here many of the restaurants and sidewalk cafés keep late hours and feature folk singers or other attractions. Just north of the **Visitor Center** (daily 9am–5pm; tel: 800-622-8300) at Avenue B is the **Historical Museum** (Wed–Sat 10am– 4pm; tel: 619-435-7242), set in a distinctive

Right: a coveted Coronado mansion

Victorian house filled with old photographs, restaurant menus, and memorabilia about early aviation adventures on the northern part of the 'island.' A number of the local restaurants offer a dinner deal that includes a performance at either the **Coronado Playhouse** (tel: 619-435-4856) or the **Lamb's Players Theater** (tel: 619-437-0600) in the Spreckels Building. Prior reservations are required, as they are at the **Village Theater** (tel: 619-435-6161) which screens first-run movies in an old-fashioned setting.

Bicycle and Gondola Rides

The town is very well served by sports amenities. There are at least 20 public tennis courts, a swimming pool (tel: 619-522-7342) at Strand Way and 15 miles (24km) of flat and scenic cycling paths. This is a great place for cyclists. Not only is there a selection of four stores from which you can rent your choice of bicycle (racer, mountain bike, tandem) but passengers are permitted to bring their two-wheeler on local buses and ferries, so you can travel some distance without compromising your independence. If you're after something less energetic, from Loews Coronado Bay Resort & Marina, you can cruise the adjoining waterways on a gondola (tel: 619-221-2999).

The red-roofed, turreted **Hotel del Coronado** (tel: 800-468-3533), which featured in Billy Wilder's 1959 movie *Some Like It Hot*, starring Marilyn

Monroe, Tony Curtis, and Jack Lemmon, is a wonderful example of elegant Victorian (1888) architecture. The hotel was founded by Elisha Babcock Jr and Hampton L Story, who used to hunt and fish on the deserted island at a time when it had more jackrabbits than San Diego had people. Even after the hotel was built, it was not unusual for a guest to go out and bag some quail, rabbit, or other small game for the chef to prepare for dinner. The founding couple's names now adorn a terrace bar, the actual 45-ft (14-m) mahogany bar of which was brought from Philadelphia by boat in 1888. *Some Like It Hot*, and other films featuring the hotel, are frequently shown on closed-circuit TV. The first movie featuring the 'hotel Del' was the 1927 silent, *The Flying Fleet*, starring Ramon Novarro and Anita Page.

The Chart House restaurant opposite looks like a miniature version of the hotel – in fact it was an early 'test model' which was built by the architects before they started work on the real thing. The Glorietta Bay Inn situated just across the street was the mansion that John D Spreckels built to be his home, apparently without a kitchen because he enjoyed the hotel's cooking so much.

Edward VIII Meets Mrs Simpson

Almost from the beginning, a rail spur on the hotel property enabled wealthy visitors to accommodate their private rail cars which, on arrival, were unhitched from the trains that had hauled them from – in most instances – the East Coast. A dozen US presidents have been guests since Thomas Edison personally turned on the electric lighting. And Britain's Edward VIII (then the Prince of Wales) met his future wife, the notorious Mrs Simpson, in the fern and palm-fringed garden where she was living in a bungalow. Charles Lindbergh dropped by before taking off from the US Naval Air Station at the northern part of the island for his transatlantic flight, and author L Frank Baum is said to have used the hotel as an inspiration for his 1900 *The Wonderful Wizard of Oz*. All these figures are recalled in a lower-level history-gallery corridor lined with fascinating photographs.

Legends persist about supernatural occurrences in rooms 3502 and 3312, which were occupied by Kate Morgan, a 27-year-old card shark, and her maid during a five-day stay in 1892. The story goes that, while supposedly waiting for her husband and gambling partner, Ms Morgan strayed to the beach where she was found shot with a gun beside her. Though her death was officially ruled to be a suicide, there was much speculation that she had been murdered, possibly by her husband, and that the maid (who disappeared, never to be heard from again) had witnessed the killing. Since then, a number of guests and staff have reported experiencing flickering lights, odd scents and unexplained voices emanating from the two rooms. For more information on this fascinating hotel, take a $15 tour (Mon–Thurs mornings, Sun afternoons; tel: 619-435-6611).

Above Left: *Some Like It Hot* was shot here
Right: a catch from the sea off Coronado

3. The Zoo and Balboa Park (see map, p31)

Today's the day for a ride on one of the bright orange-and-green trackless downtown trolleys that run every half hour.

Despite its name, **Old Town Trolley Tours** (tel: 619-298-8687) actually cover a loop between Balboa Park and Coronado. You can board and buy a ticket at any of the eight stops and get off and on at any of the others until you have completed a round trip. The last trolley from the zoo to downtown is at 5.25pm, and from downtown to the zoo at 5.40pm (4.40 in winter). If you are driving, you might want to take advantage of the zoo's free parking lot, especially given that a zoo employee sitting in a tower and armed with a pair of binoculars, will help you find your car if you misplace it in the enormous lot.

More than 4,000 animals, including rare giant pandas and the largest koala colony outside Australia live in naturalistic habitats behind moats in the lush, semitropical landscape of **San Diego Zoo** (daily 9am–9pm; tel: 619-234-3153). Indeed, many reckon that this is the best zoo in the whole country. Posted on a board near the entrance are the day's highlights, which sometimes include information about new or novel events. It's easy to get around the zoo, on pathways around the upper mesas (elephants, reptiles, elk) and lower canyons (bears, camels, tigers). There are kangaroo bus tours ('hop on and off at eight locations') or you could board a **Skyfari Aerial Tram** which affords a pleasant overhead trip but doesn't offer views of the actual animals.

Expensive Pandas

The 35-minute guided bus trip, on the other hand, takes you past camels, elephants, deer, gazelle, buffalo, polar bears, buffalo, giraffes, and species that most people have never heard of, such as takin, eland, quoll, and Russian shija. There are long lines for seats on the upper deck of the bus, shorter ones for the lower deck, from which you can see all the aforementioned creatures, but obviously from a lower perspective. Escalators ascend from the biggest attraction – the pandas, rented from China for a reported $1 million a year each. In 1999 Hua Mei became the first panda born in the Western hemisphere in a decade.

Large crowds also gather at the **Polar Bear Plunge** by the Skyfari terminal. Look through a 10-ft (3-m) high window to see these playful beasts cavorting in an Olympic-sized swimming pool whose temperature is maintained at 65°F (18°C). From a tank at the top of the rocks, fish are poured down a chute into the pool. Other favorite bear snacks are hidden in underwater rock niches. The pool, fed by a stream and a waterfall, is separated by a deep, 15-ft (4.5-m) wide moat from a hillside on which herds of Siberian reindeer graze. Misters planted unobtrusively among the cedar and juniper trees keep the area cool and moist.

Above: pandas are the zoo's most popular attraction

In another innovative adaptation of modern technology, the zoo has hidden 144 stereo speakers along the walkways in **Gorilla Tropics.** The speakers transmit sounds recorded on location in the wilds of Africa and, together with the native plants, help to authenticate this replica of a rainforest. Around a bend of the winding trail a family of life-size gorilla statues, sculpted in bronze by the artist Bob Berry, offers a popular photo opportunity.

Similarly, the 65-ft (20-m) high Rain Forest Aviary simulates the sights and sounds of a southeast Asian jungle environment with indigenous ferns, foliage, and flowers. Every day there are two sea lion shows, and two 'predators and prey' attractions. A handful of stores sell food, camera film, toys and souvenirs; and there are half a dozen eateries. The 100-acre (40-ha) grounds are like a tropical garden full of orchids, palms, ferns, and figs. A delightful **Children's Zoo** features fluffy creatures, tortoise races, and, in the animal nursery, calves, cubs and the like being cared for by their human 'mothers.'

'Museum Street'

It's only a short walk from the zoo to the museum district, although you can take the Old Town trolley, which stops at both. In addition to trolleys, Metropolitan Transit System (tel: 619-233-3004) buses (Nos 1, 3, 7, and 25) cover the journey from downtown to Balboa Park. If you're up for a stroll, pass the miniature railroad and carousel, the **Spanish Village Art Center** (where craftsmen work 11am–4pm in a complex of tiny cottages), the Moreton Bay fig tree, and the **Natural History Museum** (tel: 619-232-38210), which is home to a number of desert creatures. You are now on El Prado, the main 'museum street'.

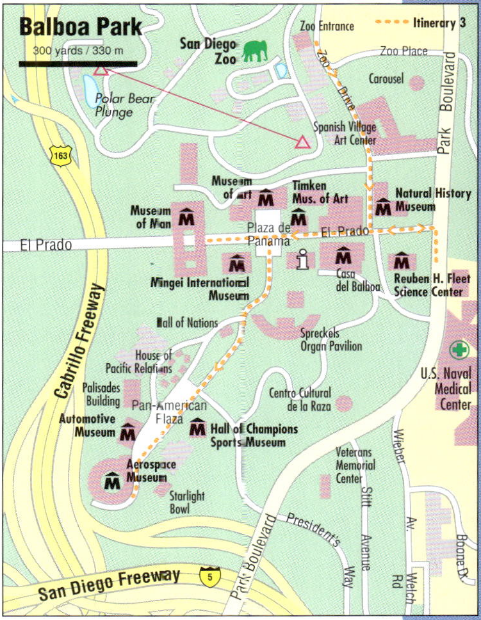

Beginning with a 609-ft (185-m) high torrent of water from a dramatic fountain, El Prado ends with the **California Tower** (part of the 'California Quadrangle') whose tile-crowned dome has become the city's logo. The 100-bell carillon chimes every quarter hour. The

Above: Old Town trolley and driver

House of Hospitality on the left houses a Visitors Center that is full of maps and relevant information. Look out for a Moorish-style restaurant, the Café del Rey Moro, which has an outdoor patio. You are now at **Balboa Park**. In 1789, Spain's King Carlos III ordered the present-day site of the park to be reserved for the people for 'pasturage or for recreational purposes.'

The beautiful white buildings that, with their red tile roofs, towers, and domes, form a highly impressive ceremonial entrance to the park, were built in the Spanish-Moorish style by Bertram Goodhue for the Panama-California International Exposition of 1915. The exposition would have been a very different story if the much admired San Diego architect Irving Gill had been selected for the project. 'The fact that San Diego has something approaching a unity of style is due entirely to Gill, whose work was so extensive and so widely copied by contractors and various draftsmen who had been through his office', wrote Esther McCoy in her book *Five California Architects* '(but) the Churrigueresque style of the buildings, with their concentration of ornament, ushered in a period… in which there was little appreciation of Gill's austere simplicity.' The 1915 exposition celebrated the completion of the Panama Canal; then, 20 years later, the buildings were refurbished for the California-Pacific Exposition. They have been an object of local pride ever since. Behind the Lily Pond the enormous Botanical Building, which contains several hundred tropical plants, may be the coolest place in the entire park.

It would take all day to appreciate the contents of the 15 museums that flank the broad Prado, but you're unlikely to decide to visit all of them. Most open at 10am, closing at 4 or 4.30pm. But you might want to check out the fine **Museum of Art** (tel: 619-232-7931), whose 16th-century Spanish-style facade is as attractive as anything inside; the **Mingei International Museum** (tel: 619-239-0003) specializing in folk art; the **Model Railroad Museum** (tel: 800-446-8738); the **Historical Society Museum** (tel: 619-232-6203), which has files containing some two million photographs; and the **Museum of Photographic Arts** (tel: 619-238-7559). All are closed on Mondays.

The other museums are open daily. See the **Museum of Man** (tel: 619-239-

Above: Balboa Park's Lily Pond
Right: the Mingei International Museum

2001) with its tiled dome; the **Timken Museum of Art** (tel: 619-239-5548); and the **Reuben H Fleet Science Center** (tel: 619-238-1233), featuring an array of hands-on exhibits as well as the world's first OMNIMAX – forerunner of IMAX – theater. The 75-ft (23-m) screen covers most of the dome and convincingly transports viewers under the ocean and into space.

Also open daily are the **Automotive Museum** (tel: 619-231-2386), whose 60 vehicles include an 1896 Benz and a 1948 Tucker; the **Hall of Champions Sports Museum** (tel: 619-234-2544) which honors the nation's winning athletes; and the **Aerospace Museum** (tel: 619-234-8291), all of which are elsewhere in the park, south of El Prado. The circular Aerospace Museum, which includes a 900-seat theater, is big enough to accommodate more than 60 aircraft – some original, some reproductions. Among them are an early model of the primitive flying machine which raised the Wright Brothers off the ground at Kitty Hawk in North Carolina in 1903, and one of two local replicas of the *Spirit of St Louis* in which, in 1927, Charles Lindbergh made the first solo crossing of the Atlantic. (The other replica is at San Diego International Airport; the original is in Washington DC.)

Freezing Actors

Most of the museums have adjoining stores that sell books, videos and appropriate souvenirs. The **Old Globe Theatre Gift Shop** (tel: 619-235-2268) behind the Museum of Man stays open until 9.30pm when there are performances at the adjacent theater, which is the oldest in California. Here, and in the outdoor Lowell Davie Festival Theater, and also at the 225-seat Cassius Carter Center Stage, there are performances on most summer evenings. The park is situated under a major flight path – a sentry at the open-air theater brandishes a flashlight with an orange beam to warn of an approaching airplane. When he flashes a red light, the actors 'freeze', and resume their performance only when the light turns green.

A free tram runs around the park – one of its stops is in the main parking lot near the Mingei museum. The Old Town trolley also stops here but,

Above: relaxing after a visit to the wonderful Reuben H Fleet Science Center

before taking a ride on it you might want to walk south to see some of the park's other attractions. These include the **Spreckels Organ Pavilion** (tel: 619-702-8138), whose gates open on Sunday afternoons (and in summer on some weekend evenings) for a concert on the world's largest outdoor pipe organ. The organ has more than 4,000 individual pipes, ranging from 33ft (10m) in length to some as short as 1 inch (2.5cm).

Nearby are the **Japanese Friendship Garden** (daily 10am–4pm; tel: 619-232-2780), which features a koi pond, wisteria arbor, and Bonsai trees, and Palm Canyon, which has 58 different species of palm tree. Southwest of Palm Canyon, the **House of Pacific Relations** group of cottages**,** each decorated in their national style, stage craft exhibitions with entertainment and samples of ethnic food on Sunday afternoons in summer and fall. Just outside the main park entrance, across I-163, is the 1905 **Marston House** (Fri–Sun 10am–4.30pm; tel: 619-298-3142), an arts and crafts mansion built by San Diego Historical Society founder George Marston.

The northeast corner of the park is devoted to sports enthusiasts: the Florida Canyon Nature Trail is enjoyed by numerous cyclists and hikers, and the Morley Field Sports Complex has tennis courts, a pool, an archery range, and various playgrounds. The public golf course (tel: 619-570-1234) is one of 50 in the county.

A Touch of Hollywood

Return to the main plaza to catch an Old Town trolley. The drivers intersperse their comments with fragments of soundtrack: the sound of an organ accompanies the passing of the Spreckels Organ, a chorus sung by Marilyn Monroe plays when outside the Hotel del Coronado. Voices imitating Groucho Marx, Clint Eastwood, Jimmy Stewart, Ronald Reagan, and Humphrey Bogart issue warnings about staying seated and keeping one's arms inside the bus.

Above: the Spreckels Organ Pavilion
Left: slam dunk, Hall of Champions Sports Museum

4. OLD TOWN *(see map, p36)*

A full day spent exploring 'Old Town', the site of the first European settlement on the West Coast.

Old Town is where in 1769 Father Junipero Serra founded the Mission San Diego de Alcala, the first of 21 missions in upper California. A few years later, the mission was moved 6 miles (9km) east to Mission Valley where there was a better water supply. The original presidio (garrison), the first European settlement on the West Coast, served as the base for Spanish explorations of the interior. Between 1825 and 1829 the Mexican governor lived in an adobe house on the site. In 1929 a local philanthropist financed the **Junipero Serra Museum** (Tues–Sat 10am–4pm, Sun noon–4pm; tel: 619-297-3258), whose hilly surroundings he enhanced by purchasing the property that is now Presidio Park and landscaping it with thousands of trees and shrubs. The museum concentrates on the pre-United States of America era of local history, and it offers a fine view from its tower.

Free one-hour tours of Old Town start from **Seeley Stables** at 11am and 2pm daily. The Stables double as a **Visitors Center** (tel: 619-220-5422) outside of which mariachis (street bands) and dancers provide entertainment on weekends. Glassblowers, potters, and diamond cutters pursue their trade in the Bazaar del Mundo, a collection of colorful stores and eateries on the north side of the plaza. There is ample free parking in Old Town, which also has lots of bus lines, and the Old Town trolley (tel: 619-298-8687).

On Wednesdays and Saturdays a group called the Old Town Boosters (tel: 619-237-6770) organizes 'living history' demonstrations of such traditional activities as brick- and candle-making, bread-baking in primitive ovens and the production of salsa and tortillas in La Casa de Machado y Silvas on the plaza.

The **Old Town Plaza** is where, in 1846, Kit Carson helped to raise the first American flag. According to legend, fights staged here between bulls and bears gave rise to the terms used for stock market trends – the bear swipes downwards, the bull hooks upwards. At one side of the plaza is the1830 adobe, **Casa de Estudillo**, once the home of the presidio commander and one of the square's seven original buildings. A group of stores and houses on the plaza's south side includes the former home of Richard Freeman and Allen B Light, the first Afro-Americans to settle in the town. On the corner, the **Colorado House**, now housing a Wells Fargo museum, once served as a hotel.

Farther along San Diego Avenue a wood-frame structure (shipped from Maine) has been restored to look as it did in 1868, when the first edition of

Right: the Casa de Estudillo is one of the Old Town plaza's original buildings

the *San Diego Union* was printed here. The rival *San Diego Herald* was headquartered in the **Robinson-Rose House** at the west side of the plaza.

On Calhoun Street, which runs parallel, you can see a couple of the old Concord coaches that Albert Seeley operated on his stagecoach line to Los Angeles in the late 1860s at Seeley Stables *(see page 35)*. Traveling at about 5mph (8kph) and changing horses every three hours, the 130-mile (210-km), largely uncomfortable trip took 24 hours, barring accidents. In the words of the writer Bret Harte: 'Lunatics had not yet reached such imbecility as to ride of their own free will in California's stages'. Seeley, a former Illinois farm boy who grew up with Ulysses S Grant, did very well from the line. One of the Old Town elite, Seeley was vociferously skeptical about the town that was Alonzo Horton's new enterprise, and boasted: 'Your mushroom town will soon peter out and the people will [still] have to come to Old Town to take the stage'. Within a few years, however, the Southern Pacific Railroad arrived and the stagecoach line became obsolete.

La Casa de Bandini, built in 1829, was the home of Governor Pio Pico's secretary, Juan Bandini. Financial losses incurred by a cattle ranch and other businesses forced Bandini to sell his fine home (to a Frenchman named Adolph Savin) for $600. The property had been turned into an olive-pickling factory by the time it was bought by Seeley, who added a second story and transformed it into the Cosmopolitan Hotel. 'The rooms of the hotel are large and well ventilated and finely furnished,' he advertised. 'The table will always be supplied with all the delicacies of the season and no pains will be spared to make guests comfortable during their stay.' Now owned by the state of California, it is an attractive restaurant specializing in fine Mexican cuisine. Behind the building you'll find an old blacksmith's shop where volunteers occasionally demonstrate the trade's traditional techniques.

Numerous other Old Town restaurants serve Mexican fare. One of the best is the **Casa de Pico** (tel: 619-296-3267) in the Bazaar del Mundo.

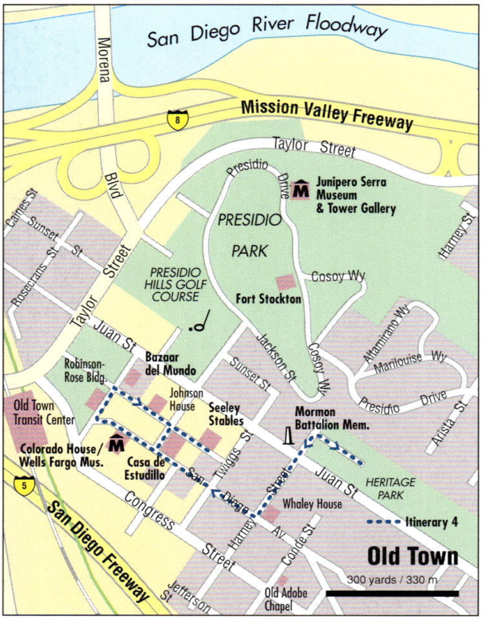

Lincoln's Mask

Other interesting sites in Old Town include the 1856 **Whaley House**. This, the oldest brick building in San Diego, was once the courthouse and is reputed to be haunted. Among its exhibits is a life-mask of Abraham Lincoln (who sat for it in 1860). Of the six that were made, the only other survivor is in Washington DC's Smithsonian Museum. Behind the Whaley House is the **Derby Pendleton House**, erected here in 1851, after arriving by boat from Maine.

The classroom of the **Mason Street School** is lined with photos

of long-dead teachers; a stool with a dunce's cap stands in the corner. Discipline was strict when this little red schoolhouse was built in 1865. 'Fighting at school, 5 lashes; boys and girls playing together, 4 lashes; coming to school with dirty hands and faces, 2 lashes' reads the sign.

The long, heroic march undertaken by Mormon volunteers to fight in the Mexican-American war is commemorated in the **Mormon Battalion Visitors Center** (daily 9am–9pm; tel: 619-298-3317) where a short movie recounts the story of the 500 volunteers recruited in 1846. Their 2,000-mile (3,200-km) trek from Iowa to join the US Army in California is celebrated as the longest-ever infantry march. Farther up the hill is **Heritage Park** where many Victorian buildings are preserved, along with San Diego's first synagogue.

Design a Teddy Bear

Not everything in Old Town is old. At the **Basic Brown Bear Factory** (tel: 877-234-2327) on San Diego Avenue you can design, stuff and dress your own teddy bear from over 30 models and scores of outfits. If you're in Old Town for the evening you might check out the little Twiggs Street Theater (tel: 619-688-2492) where the musical comedy *Forever Plaid* pays good-natured tribute to 1950s and 1960s harmony groups.

East of Old Town are Mission Valley's homes and shopping centers, and on Mission Road the **San Diego de Alcala** (daily 9am–5pm; tel: 619-281-8449). This, the first mission established by Father Serra in San Diego, was moved here in 1769. Native American laborers cultivated wheat, barley, corn, and beans here 50,000as well as tending vegetable gardens and orchards; by 1797 the mission had constructed an extensive irrigation system and was cultivating 50,000 acres (20,000ha). The present building, which replaced one destroyed by an earthquake in 1803, was reconstructed in the 1940s. Among the artifacts in the museum are notes in Father Serra's handwriting.

Above: the Presidio Park museum focuses on local history
Right: commemorating Mormon heroism in the Mexican war

5. Point Loma & Cabrillo Monument *(see map below)*

A morning exploring the beautiful Point Loma peninsula.

Starting at the Old Town Transit Center, take bus No 26 down the Point Loma peninsula to visit the beautiful site of the Cabrillo National Monument.

Point Loma, the peninsula on the west side of San Diego Harbor, confusingly refers to both the peninsula and the town on its eastern shore. From the days when the Spanish built an adobe fort here it has been significant militarily – look out for abandoned bunkers, gun battery positions, and the remains of other defense installations. Today much of the peninsula is devoted to Fort Rosecrans Military Reservation which incorporates a US Naval supply center and also military cemeteries. Between Rosecrans Street and the airport, the **Naval Training Center** (Mon–Fri 8am–4pm; tel: 619-524-4210) invites drive-through tours; you can see a Recruit Review at 1.15pm on Fridays. Admission is via Gate 1 on Lytton Street.

The northern end of the peninsula is now largely residential. It was here, in 1896, that Katherine A Tingley arrived to build a mansion she called The Homestead as a school for 'the Revival of the Lost Mysteries of Antiquity,' ie, the teaching of Eastern mysticism. Eventually 50 all-white buildings were occupied by the Universal Brotherhood and Theosophical Society which, like most utopian communities, declined into a cult accused of financial irregularities and alienation of affection. Ms Tingley died abroad in 1929 and the site became the property of the California Western University.

If you are driving, take any of the roads that head south to Catalina Avenue (SR 239) which

leads down to the tip of the peninsula 4 miles (6km) away. The latter stretch travels through gloriously unspoilt terrain of gorse and other greenery. From the Old Town Transit Center, bus No 26 follows this route.

At the end of the road, the 140-acre (60-ha) **Cabrillo National Monument** (daily 9am–5pm; tel: 619-557-5450) celebrates the day in 1542 when Juan Rodriguez Cabrillo stepped ashore here and claimed the territory for the Spanish Crown. A 'birthday celebration' takes place during the last week of September every year. The Visitors Center displays a Fresnel lens of the type used in the nearby lighthouse, and a wonderful selection of books. There are daily screenings of movies and slide shows and a historical exhibit detailing the food found on ships in Cabrillo's day (olive oil, dried fish, beans, hardtack, wine). Outside, powerful telescopes magnify views of Coronado and the bay area. This is a popular place from which to watch the scores of whales that pass by in January and February.

Farther up the hill, atop a delightful two-story house that rises 460ft (140m) above the sea, is a lighthouse. Two tiny bedrooms above a kitchen, dining area and sitting room were shared by two families in the days (1855–1891) when the kerosene-fueled light guided boats home. At that time the supplies had to be heaved along a rugged, 10-mile (16-km) trail from San Diego.

The Last Lighthouse Keeper

Captain Robert Israel, who served 18 years, was the last of 11 keepers, few of whom lasted more than a year in the cramped quarters on a miserly $800 per-annum salary. 'Life is lonely here,' noted Maria Israel. 'Captain Israel and his family fill the quiet hours reading, making crafts from shells and seaweed like the frame for the picture over the fireplace, or tend to lighthouse duties.' Eventually the lighthouse, whose beam was often obscured by clouds or fog, was replaced by one at a lower level.

In its earlier days it was known as 'the Spanish light' although the only Spanish light was the lantern hung on a pole in the 1770s at nearby Ballast Point as a signal to northbound supply ships. In that era a wooden building near the lighthouse was the scene of all-night dances for the mostly Spanish population. The mid-19th century was the whaling industry's heyday. Two New England whaling firms set up their headquarters at Ballast Point, a projection of land on the bay side.

Above: a friendly Cabrillo National Monument park ranger
Right: father and son undertake some rockpool investigations

From the lighthouse the 2-mile (3-km) **Bayside Trail** down to the sea is bordered with succulents, sage plants, and tall lemonadeberry shrubs from whose fruit early inhabitants made an apparently tasty drink. From the main parking lot, a drive along the shore leads to another parking lot. From here you can negotiate slippery rocks to visit the tide-pool homes of hermit crabs, sea anemones, and other little creatures. If you're driving, stop for lunch at Shelter Island, a peninsula off Point Loma's eastern shore. Or you could return to Old Town for lunch before taking the No 9 bus to Mission Bay and SeaWorld.

6. Mission Bay and SeaWorld *(see map, p38)*

Mission Bay has good beaches and plenty of family-oriented attractions.

Starting at theOld Town Transit Center take bus No 9.

The 4,600-acre (1,860-ha) **Mission Bay** area was once a swamp and is now the world's largest aquatic playground. Here parkland, beaches, and numerous inner lagoons offer lots of wet recreation. There are free launching ramps at marinas and park hotels and berthing facilities for more than 2,000 boats. At Quivira Basin boats can anchor free for 72 hours; the De Anza Bay resort is reserved for campers and recreational vehicles. The area around Tecolote Shores is a quiet field where people fly kites. For a cruise with dinner, drinks, and dancing, the sternwheeler *Bahia Belle* (tel: 858-488-0551) departs from the Bahia, Catamaran, and Paradise Point hotels (Wed to Sat nights; Fri, Sat in winter).

The Mission Bay beaches are a major attraction for out-of-state tourists, especially those from Arizona (who form 12 percent of San Diego's visitors), but the owner of a local sports shop says they 'always seem to be ill-

Above: Cabrillo National Monument tide pools
Left: traditional carousel at Belmont Park

prepared for the temperate climate.' San Diego summer temperatures – usually in the 80s Fahrenheit (high 20s– low 30s Centigrade) – are at least 25°F (14°C) cooler than those in Phoenix.

Mission Bay is flanked by I-5 in the east and Mission Boulevard on the ocean side. It's bordered by Grand Avenue at the northern end and the San Diego River to the south. If you don't have a car, the No 9 bus from Old Town Transit Center runs all the way up to Pacific Beach past **Belmont Park** (daily; tel: 619-491-2988). You can't miss the park: its giant rollercoaster, built in 1925, soars across 2,600ft (790m) of track. En route the bus stops at **SeaWorld** (opens 9am in summer, 10am in winter, closing times vary; tel: 619-226-3901) – a 150-acre (61-ha) marine zoo.

Killer whales, such as the 4,500lb (2,000kg) Shamu, are the biggest stars at SeaWorld. Their performances invariably pack the 5,000-seat stadium. They leap into the air to amazing heights, speed through the water with their keepers on their backs, and take turns in whacking the water with their huge tails to soak visitors sitting in the front rows. (There's never a shortage of volunteers for this whale-induced shower). SeaWorld is known for rehabilitating sickly sea creatures; in 1998 it returned to the ocean an orphaned gray whale, JJ, that had arrived in a distressed state the previous year.

Pirates and Rapids

The thrice-daily Sea Lion and Otter Show is irresistibly amusing, as are the dolphins, and a teeming mass of hundreds of penguins that swim underwater. Friendly dolphins can be petted. Pirates 4-D is an in-your-face movie experience with watery effects, viewed through special 3-D eyeglasses. In Shipwreck Rapids, participants start as island castaways and negotiate their way back to civilization via raging rapids, roaring waterfalls and a near collision with a ship's propeller. At the so-called Beer School, where Clydesale horses can be admired, Budweiser offers free samples until 4pm. A panoramic view of the area can be seen from the **Sky Tower**, which revolves as it rises 330ft (98m) before coming straight down. If you are here in spring, you could join one of SeaWorld's guided whale-watching trips off the coast.

Just to the north is **Paradise Point Resort** on Vacation Island. This somewhat secluded upscale facility features suites opening onto soft, white beaches, a heated swimming pool, sailboats and bicycles for rent, and a guided boat tour. It's a pleasant place to stay but even if you're not a guest, you might like to stop off here for a drink at the Barefoot Bar & Grill, which has good food and often live music. On Sunday mornings, the themed Beatles Brunch includes a screening of *Yellow Submarine* in the Sand Room.

South of the channel is **Ocean Beach,** formerly a mecca for Old Town gourmets who knew it as Mussel Beach. To the north is **Pacific Beach** where

Above: youngsters love to play with the dolphins

activities tend to center on Crystal Pier or the area along Mission Boulevard up Garnet Avenue where the locals shop and dine. All three beaches attract sun-seekers during most of the year. Humphrey's Half Moon Inn, a waterfront restaurant on Shelter Island, offers live music every night. Between Shelter Island with its **Pacific Rim Park** (tel: 760-436-3960) and Harbor Island, at the northern side of the bay, is America's Cup Harbor. The artificial islands feature parks, fishing facilities, restaurants, and yacht clubs.

When you're ready for dinner, head back downtown to the lively Gaslight District for a meal at **Croce's** (5th & F streets, tel: 619-233-4355) The restaurant's owner, Ingrid, married Jim Croce in 1966, and took the title of her cookbook, *Thyme in a Bottle* (on sale at Croce's) from the late singer's big hit, *Time in a Bottle.* Before moving to San Diego in 1973, the couple grew vegetables and baked bread in a Pennsylvania farmhouse, cooking for musicians such as Arlo Guthrie, Bonnie Raitt and James Taylor. Croce died in a plane crash in September 1973.

7. LA JOLLA *(see map, p43)*

This lovely seashore town offers great beaches, an excellent aquarium and wonderful coastal trails.

Take bus No 30 or 34 from the Plaza in downtown San Diego.

The charming coastal community of **La Jolla** (pronounced 'La-Hoy-Ya'), one of the country's most affluent zip codes, is 14 miles (23km) north of San Diego. With its clifftop location and access via a winding road, it could be mistaken for one of the towns of the French Riviera. Complementing La Jolla's beautiful homes is a downtown area known as 'the village' that's filled with expensive stores (and a contemporary art museum). Shopping on Prospect Street, a Rodeo Drive clone, is the main preoccupation: a visitors' guide produced by the local paper devotes two-thirds of its space to the subject, along with a map showing parking lots (free if accompanied by a store's validation). A rt exhibitions are a downtown feature on the first Thursday evening of each month.

Once described by mystery writer

Above: Crystal Pier on Pacific Beach
Right: Museum of Contemporary Art

Raymond Chandler as 'a nice place for old people and their parents,' La Jolla featured in Tom Wolfe's 1960s surfer novel *The Pump House Gang*. On the campus of the University of California is the La Jolla Playhouse whose forerunner was founded by local actor Gregory Peck. The caves carved into its coastal bluffs have long been a paradise for both skin divers and cliff divers and nearby **Black's Beach** was once legally – and is now illegally – a nudist beach. There are 33 beaches spread along the county's coastline.

The **Museum of Contemporary Art** (Tues–Sat 10am–5pm, Sun noon–5; tel: 858-454-3541), with its fabulous Pacific views framed by picture windows, was originally itself a work of art. A modest home built for Ellen Browning Scripps by Irving Gill (1870–1936), it exemplified Gill's philosophy: 'We should build our house simple, plain and substantial as a boulder, then leave the ornamentation of it to Nature, who will tone it with lichens, chisel it with storms, make it gracious and friendly with vines and flower shadows as she does the stone in the meadow.'

Ms Scripps's brothers founded the *Detroit Tribune* where she was a proofreader in 1867. She later became a columnist for the family's *Detroit Evening News* before moving to San Diego and commissioning the house which, after her death, became La Jolla's Art Center. When it was enlarged and modified, Gill's facade and his signature arched entry were removed.

Exploring Realms of Knowledge

The media tycoon E W Scripps opened the Scripps Institute, whose function he explained thus: 'Endowed colleges, governmental institutions, and most of the other institutions of research are affected by personal prejudices and partisan interests. Too many of them are founded upon crass ignorance and even carelessness of any other purpose than that of profiting by fame or by salaries or other ignoble considerations… I wish to gather together at this institution a number of men of strong minds who are eager for research work, eager to penetrate the, as yet, unexplored realms of knowledge.'

Today, the renowned Scripps Institute of Oceanographic Research is acclaimed for its research facilities and its well-stocked **Stephen Birch Aquarium** (daily 9am–5pm; tel: 858-534-3474) on Expedition Way just north of town offers whale-watching cruises in season. Among the 33 seawater tanks is a two-story affair that copies a kelp bed off the coast with all its familiar and unfamiliar creatures, while another environment replicates the ocean off Baja. Visitors can watch fish feeding sessions at 1.30pm on Wednesdays and Sundays. From the hilltop plaza, the view is of the coastline and the private pier below, from which the institute's shorter expeditions depart, and where diving and research practices are explained.

The exhibit Exploring the Blue Planet, extends over seven self-contained areas, each dealing with a different aspect of the oceans' environmental importance: how seawater moves as currents, tides and waves; how the ocean interacts with the atmosphere to determine the weather, and how shifts in the seabed can result in earthquakes and volcanoes. You can experience a simulated submersible ride that illustrates the diverse forms of marine life, from the ocean's surface to the inky depths.

A series of participatory adventures includes coastal walks, 'tidepooling,' and moonlit hunts for the grunion fish which, under state law, can be caught only with bare hands. The aquarium has won awards for its sea horse propagation program – it is the first such aquarium in the country to raise successive generations of the delightful little *hippocampus ingens*, hundreds of which it has distributed to facilities worldwide.

La Jolla Shores Drive leads to Torrey Pines Road. This winding hill out of La Jolla passes through the affluent suburb of Torrey Pines, where the distinctive trees that grow only here and on the island of Santa Rosa are officially protected. Steep trails run down the hillside to the beach at whose northern end is Los Penasquitos Lagoon, which is known for its excellent bird-watching. The highlight of Torrey Pines Road however is the architecturally awesome **Salk Institute** (weekday tours by appointment, tel: 858-453-4100), designed by the late Louis I Kahn, who many consider to be America's finest 20th-century architect. The institute is named for its resident scientist Jonas Salk, who developed the polio vaccine.

Gliders Over the Ocean

Atop the mesa off Park Road, you will find the **Visitors Center** (tel: 858-755-2063) in an Indian-style adobe structure which incorporates a museum. From Park Road there is access to Torrey Pines Scenic Drive. From here you can see the windswept hillside from which flying enthusiasts have been launching gliders over the ocean since the 1930s. The **Torrey Pines Gliderport** (tel: 888-452-9858) offers introductory lessons in paragliding and hangliding. There's a restaurant and store at the site.

Take Genessee Road (State Highway 21) to connect with I-5 heading north. A superlative panoramic view of both coast and inland can be found atop the 820-ft (250-m) high **Mount Soledad** in Soledad Natural Park near the junction of Ardath and Torrey Pines roads. (The Garnet Street exit from I-5 leads to Soledad Mountain Road). For years a heated controversy has surrounded the cross that stands at the summit of this city-owned site, but there can be little disagreement about the superlative panoramic views from the top.

Left: cliff face at Torrey Pines

8. Del Mar (see map, p43)

This evening in Del Mar makes is an enjoyable extension to itinerary 7.

The beachside community of Del Mar has been enticing crowds since the 1930s. It is only a short distance beyond Torrey Pines and is served by an AMTRAK station. You could dine at one of the six restaurants in **Del Mar Plaza**, between the racetrack and Scripps Institute, enjoying a splendid view of the ocean while you eat. The following are recommended: Kitima (tel: 619-792-7000) for Thai cuisine; Pacifica del Mar (tel: 619-792-0476) for seafood; or Enotica del Fornaio (tel: 858-755-8639) for Italian. The plaza is full of art galleries and gift shops. The **Del Mar Fairgrounds** (tel: 858-755-1161) at the intersection of I-5 and Via de la Valle feature all sorts of weird and wonderful events, from monster truck racing to dog and bird shows. On the main street, you can view, touch and even buy million-year-old fossils at the **Dinosaur Gallery** (daily 11am–5pm; tel: 858-794-4855). Several companies offering balloon flights are stationed in Del Mar.

Racetrack Rescue

Del Mar's racetrack was rescued from bankruptcy by actor Pat O'Brien and singer Bing Crosby, who turned it into one of the country's most popular racing circuit venues. The season begins in July, a week after the big fair ends, and continues through mid-September. The track's sand-colored main building can be seen from the pseudo-Tudor stores on the highway up the hill.

About 5 miles (8km) to the east of Del Mar off I-5 along County Highway S6 is **Rancho Santa Fe**. In this affluent country-style answer to Beverly Hills, the powerful residents' association dictates even what kind of flowers can be grown. It first became a popular retreat among Hollywood celebrities in the late 1920s when Douglas Fairbanks and his wife, Mary Pickford, built their Fairbanks Ranch here. Other movie stars who later built plush homes on the tree-covered slopes of Rancho Santa Fe include Victor Mature, Robert Young, and Patti Page.

Above: the 'Love Bus' captures the fun flavor of Del Mar

Excursions

1. Carlsbad and Oceanside (see maps, p48 and 49)

The 25 miles (48km) of beaches stretching from Del Mar northwards to Oceanside are a major attraction.

The beaches running north of Del Mar offer wonderful opportunities for two- or three-day hikes, and are well served by a variety of eateries and places to stay. And, if the hike leaves you feeling tired, you can always hop onto one of the buses that run constantly up and down the coast road.

After passing through Solana Beach and Cardiff, it's worth a stop in Encinitas to see the **Quail Botanical Gardens** (daily 9am–5pm; tel:760-436-3036) which have a waterfall and a large collection of bamboo and hibiscus. Or you might want to check out the tranquil gardens of the **Self Realisation Fellowship** (Tues–Sat 8am–5pm; tel: 760-753-1811).

About an hour's drive from San Diego is **Carlsbad**, named after the Czech spa because the water of its early wells had similar beneficial properties. Here you can visit the nation's biggest maker of golf clubs, **Callaway Golf** (daily tours; tel: 760-931-1771). For 60 years the town's major attraction has been the **Flower Fields** (daily 10am–dusk; tel: 760-930-9123) at Palomar Airport Road off I-5. The fields attract thousands of visitors from late February through April. You can walk among masses of red, yellow, orange, and pink flowers that spread across 50 acres (20ha) of hillside in alternating bands. Persian poppies, or 'ranunculus' as the growers call them, predominate. Guides demonstrate the planting process and the growing cycle. The Bird of Paradise, first commercially developed here, is the city's official flower.

If you're not here in May and November for Carlsbad's big street fairs you might want to settle for some bird-watching, or take a leisurely stroll along the nature trail beside the **Batiquitos Lagoon** (tel: 760-943-7583), nestled between two upscale resorts (Avira and La Costa) at the south end of town.

San Diego County is known as the world's avocado capital – and if you're in Fallbrook in April you might want to check out the annual Avocado Festival. The other avocado centers are Vista, Carlsbad, and Escondido.

A Surfer Dude's Museum

Off I-5 at the northern end, another lagoon, **Buena Vista Audubon** (Tues–Sat 10am–4pm, Sun 1–4pm; tel: 760-439-BIRD) separates the town from **Oceanside** and the **California Surf Museum** (daily 10am–4pm; closed Tues in fall and winter; tel: 760-721-6876). The museum is run by surf veteran Rich Watkins who explains, 'I'm just a surfer dude who walked in and never left.' Its gift shop has a display that charts the evolution of surfboards from the 16-footers (5-m) weighing 200lbs (90kg) to today's

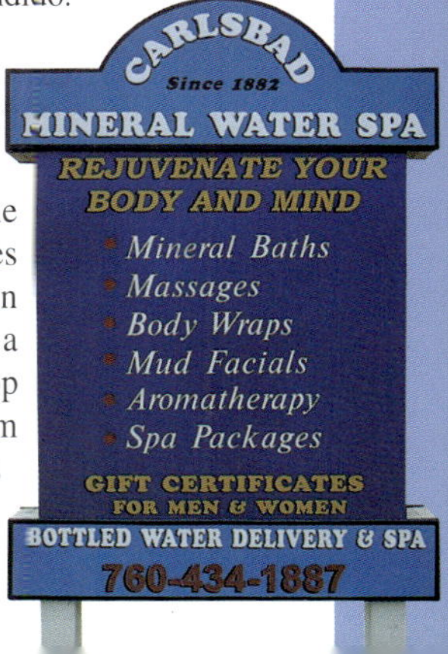

Left: the Quail Botanical Gardens in Encinitas
Right: California is the place for all sorts of rejuvenation

Norco
Prado Flood Control Basin
Woodcrest
Sunnymead
Beaumont
Banning
White Water
Moreno Valley
Edgemont
Mt Russell 2765
Cabazon
Corona
Home Gardens
Lake Perris
Jacinto River
Gilman Hot Springs
San Jacinto Mts.
Palm Springs
SAN BERNARDINO NATIONAL FOREST
Lake Matthews
El Cerrito
Lakeview
Temescal Wash
Nuevo
San Jacinto
Pine Cove
Idyllwild
Cathedral City
Estelle Mtn 2765
Homeland
Hemet
Valle Vista
Silverado
CLEVELAND NATIONAL FOREST
Alberhill
Quail Valley
Romoland
Mountain Center
Modjeska
Santiago Pk 5684
Sun City
Winchester
Polly Butte 3342
Lake Elsinore
Los Angeles
Trabuco Canyon
CALIFORNIA
Thomas Mtn 6813
Thomas Mtn.
Lakeland Village
Bachelor Mtn 2555
San Juan Hot Springs
Sitton Pk 3273
Elsmore Peak 3575
Wildomar
Sage
Cahuilla Mtn 5638
Anza
Mission Viejo
Murrieta
Cahuilla
Laguna Niguel
Mission
Oak Mtn 2706
San Juan Capistrano
Rancho California
Temecula
Vail Lake
Iron Spring Mtn 5753
Old Indian Burial Ground
Radec
Dana Point
Margarita Peak 3188
Gavilan Mtn 1830
Aguanga
Richard Nixon Library & Birthplace
De Luz
Agua Tibia Mtn 4779
ANZA-BORREGO DESERT STATE PARK
San Clemente
Camp Pendleton
Rainbow
Oak Grove
Mt Palomar 6137
Observatory
San Mateo Point
San Onofre Mtn 1725
Fallbrook
Pala
CLEVELAND N. F.
Hot Springs Mtn 6530
SAN ONOFRE STATE BEACH
Marine Corps Base
Santa Margarita River
Palomar Mtn
NAT'L FOREST
Agua Caliente
Pauma Valley
Warner Springs
Bonsall
Rincon
Las Flores
Lake Henshaw
Pala Vista
Pine Mtn 4221
Ranchita
San Luis Rey
Mission San Luis Rey de Francia
Valley Center
Morettis
Black Mtn 4051
San Felipe
Oceanside
Vista
Lake Wohlford
Mesa Grande
Volcan Mtn 5717
CARLSBAD STATE BEACH
Legoland California
Carlsbad
San Marcos
Escondido
San Diego Wild Animal Park
Santa Ysabel
Wynola
Whispering Pines
Mt Whitney 1735
San Pasqual Battlefield State Historic Park
Julian
Granite Mtn 5632
LEUCADIA STATE BEACH
Escondido Ck
Del Dios
San Pasqual
Pine Hills
Leucadia
Lake Hodges
Rancho Bernardo
Rock Haven
Ramona
Encinitas
Cuyamaca
Cardiff-by-the-Sea
Rancho Santa Fe
Rosemont
Boulder Ck
Solana Beach
Rancho Penasquitos
Barona Mesa
Cuyamaca Peak 6193
Del Mar Racetrack
Del Mar
Fernbrook
CUYAMACA RANCHO STATE PARK
TORREY PINES STATE RESERVE
Poway
Barona
El Cajon Mtn 3674
El Capitan Res.
Sorrento
San Vicente Res.
Echo Dell
Gliderport
Miramar
Descanso
Guatay
Salk Institute
Scripps Institution of Oceanography
San Diego River
Alpine
Lakeside
Stephen Birch Aquarium
La Jolla
Crest
Pine Valley
Cowles Mtn 1591
Santee
Harbison Canyon
Pacific Beach
Linda Vista
El Cajon
Loveland Res.
Pine Valley Ck
SAN DIEGO
La Mesa
Mission Beach
Spring Valley
Los Pinos Mtn 6511
Ocean Beach
PACIFIC OCEAN
Lemon Grove
San Miguel Mtn 2565
Jamul
NATIONAL FOREST
Coronado
Sweetwater Res.
Barrett Lake
Morena Village
San Diego Bay
National City
Dulzura
Dulzura Ck
Hauser Mtn 3805
CHULA VISTA
SILVER STRAND STATE BEACH
Barrett
Potrero
Otay
Lower Otay Res.
Imperial Beach
Palm City
Tecate Peak 3887
Tecate
San Ysidro
TIJUANA RIVER NATIONAL ESTUARINE SANCTUARY
Redoudo
Playas de Tijuana
TIJUANA
Matanuco
Carrizo
MEXICO
Excursions
10 miles / 16 km
Presa Rodriguez
Rio Las Palmas
Rosarito

fiber-glass 'potato chip' boards. There's a huge market among 'dudes' for surfing memorabilia and much of the museum's collection is considered to be priceless. The museum honors surfing veterans such as Olympic medal-winning swimmer Duke Kahanamoka. For lunch, you could try the Longboarder Café across the road.

Four miles (6km) inland from the beach on SR 14 is the lovely **Mission San Luis Rey de Francia** (daily 10am–4.30pm; tel: 760-757-3651). The museum here contains an 1865 document signed by Lincoln shortly before his assassination that confirms the mission's right to the land. In its heyday almost 3,000 Native Americans worked for what was the 18th of the 21 California missions. Pleasant strolls can be taken through the mission's 56 acres (23ha) of grounds. The vegetation includes the first pepper tree to be brought to the state from Peru in the mid-19th century. At nearby **Heritage Park** (park daily, buildings Sun 1–3pm; tel: 760-433-8297) the collection of century-old buildings includes the cottage that once served as Oceanside's post office.

Thirty Million Bricks

Legoland California (daily 10am–6pm; 9am–9pm in summer; tel: 760-438-LEGO), the first Legoland in the US, sprawls over 128 acres (50ha) off Cannon Road, east of I-5. Thirty million bricks are said to have gone into its construction. After seeing plastic foxes, zebras, giraffes, and the like, it's disconcerting to find real birds frisking in a stream. But there is plenty to keep the children occupied, from shooting water into the jaws of model alligators and driving electric minicars to boat rides. A series of theme 'villages' sells overpriced souvenirs and snacks. The park's highlight, a series of reproduced American cities – New York, Washington, New Orleans – with landmark buildings and moving vehicles almost redeems the tackiness of the rest of the park.

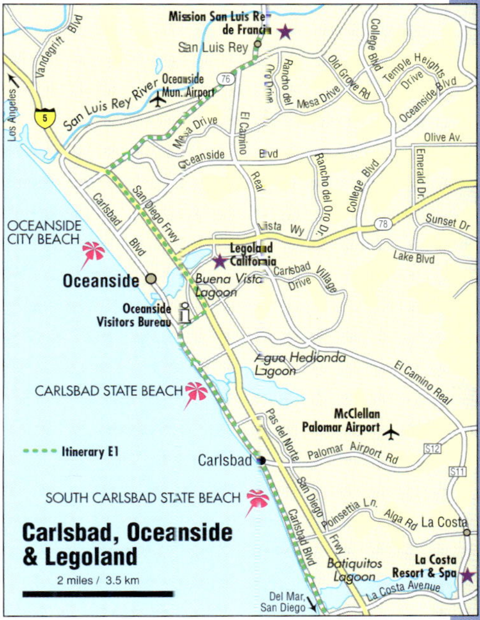

Above: Mission San Luis Rey

2. SOUTH OF THE BORDER *(see maps, p48 and 50)*

A dip into Mexico to visit the fascinating town of Tijuana.

The journey south to Mexico passes the string of suburban communities that surround the lower end of San Diego Bay. These include National City and Chula Vista, which was once part of the Rancho de la Nación where mission herds grazed, until the military took it over. Today both have growing commercial districts that depend heavily on Mexican shoppers coming across the border. The nation's first shopping center was National City's **South Bay Plaza**, which opened in 1953. This served as the prototype for an innovative type of mall that transformed American merchandising and shopping habits.

The **Chula Vista Nature Center** (Tues–Sun 10am–5pm; tel: 619-422-2473), 7 miles (11km) north of the border, has an observation deck from which you can study the hundreds of birds that gather in the surrounding salt marshes. Binoculars can be rented at the visitors center, where there are exhibits of burrowing owls and tanks of various sea creatures. Free shuttle buses run to the center from the Bayfront/E Street trolley station.

Also in Chula Vista is the **Arco Training Center** of the United States Olympic Committee. This 150-acre (60-ha) complex, which adjoins the Lower Otay Reservoir, is responsible for producing the country's future Olympic champions. From the **Copley Visitors Center** (daily; tel: 619-482-6222), which features a theater and a souvenir store, you can take a free tour along an elevated pathway to watch the nation's aspiring gold medalists working out at a variety of athletic endeavors.

Some 5 miles (8km) inland from Chula Vista's Main Street you'll find **Knotts Soak City** (daily in summer; weekends in May and Sept; tel: 619-661-7373 for opening times), where 32 'water-logged acres' (13ha) are filled with water slides that all feed into a tremendous, refreshing cool pool.

Of the two major border crossings, the eastern one is on SR 94 at **Tecate**. The California side of this community is represented by a small shopping center and post office; the Mexican side is home to a thriving community of 5,000 and the renowned Tecate brewery. There is rarely a crowd waiting to cross the border here, and there's usually just the one customs agent on duty. Be warned that he might close the border in the early evening if traffic is light.

Much busier is the **San Ysidro** border crossing. San Ysidro, a booming, bilingual community, is the busiest international border in the world – 40 million people cross the border here every year.

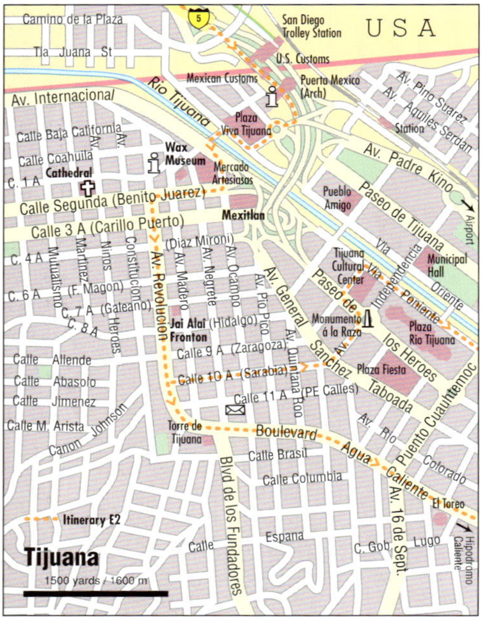

Visitors to northern Baja who stay for 72 hours or less (usually about the time needed for a roundtrip to Enseñada) don't need passports or tourist cards but if you are a resident alien in the US, remember to have your green card with you at all times. Those in this category who cannot produce the card on demand are fined on the spot – if they are allowed back into the US at all.

If you don't have a car, San Diego's red trolley cars have covered the 20-mile (32-km) trip from the Santa Fe Depot on Kettner and C streets to San Ysidro since 1981. In daytime, the trolleys to **Mexico** leave every 15 minutes for the 30-minute journey. After you disembark at the terminal, walk across the border and you'll find taxis and buses waiting to take you to downtown **Tijuana**, which is about a 10-minute drive.

If you're driving you can either park in San Ysidro and walk into Mexico, or drive through the border. The advantage of traveling by trolley is that you avoid parking hassles at the border, long lines of autos coming back to the US, and the imposition of extra auto insurance, which is advisable when driving in Mexico. You can pick up relevant information at the Tijuana Tourism and Convention Bureau **information booth** (Mon–Fri 8am–9pm, Sat 8am–10pm, Sun 8am–7pm) at the San Ysidro border crossing, and at similar booths at the Otay border crossing (daily 9am–4pm), and at Third and Revolución streets in downtown Tijuana (daily 9am–5pm).

Tia Juana (Aunt Jane)

As you drive into Tijuana or cross the footbridge you can see the impressive **Mexitlan** museum (Tues–Sun 10am–6pm; tel: 38-41-655) at Ave Benito Juarez 8991. The Mexitlan features scale reproductions of sculptures, temples, monuments, and other buildings that reflect 1,500 years of Mexican history. The 150 scale models include the Pyramid of the Sun at Teotihuacan as well as the stadium where the 1968 Olympics were held in Mexico City. The building is the work of Mexico's top architect, Pedro Ramirez Vásquez, who created Mexico City's anthropology museum. Next door is the arts and crafts market, **Mercado Artesiasas**. Walk two blocks west to the **Wax Museum** (tel: 88-24-78) at the corner of Ave Madero and Calle Iera; its 60 models include Madonna, Fidel Castro, and the legendary Tía Juana (Aunt Jane), the owner of a lively cantina (pub) around which the city was reputedly founded.

Above: Mexican handicrafts, downtown Tijuana
Right: a Mickey Mouse VW shows the impact of Hollywood

Five blocks south on Revolución at Calle Galiana, the **Jai Alai Fronton** (tel: 38-43-08) comes to life every Tues, Wed, and Thurs night when the dazzlingly fast sport of jai alai– played with a ball and wicker basket – enthralls noisy crowds, most of whom bet on their favorite player.

If you want to visit the winery (tel: 85-30-51), head for Calle Johnson at Hidalgo. The main street continues south, where it joins the Boulevard Agua Caliente, past the city's old bullring, the sports arena, which is also the venue for many big concerts, and the **Hipodromo Caliente** racetrack. Hollywood stars who used to frequent the racetrack include Charlie Chaplin, Jean Harlow, Stan Laurel, and Oliver Hardy. If you would like to check out the greyhound races that take place here every day, tel: 81-78-11.

For family entertainment, turn right on 10th Street and head east toward the broad Paseo de los Heroes and Velazco, where you'll find **Mundo Divertido** (tel: 34-32-12). This center offers mini golf, video games, bumper boats, go karts, and refreshment stands. Farther up Heroes at Calle Mina, the **Tijuana Cultural Center** (tel: 84-11-11) includes Olmec stone heads; a meticulously created model of the 16th-century capital, Tenochtitlan; a dramatic portrait of the legendary Father Miguel Hidalgo; embroidered Indian costumes and all sorts of folk art and crafts. For more modern consumer items, walk back along the river to the **Plaza Rio Tijuana Shopping Center** which, with about 100 stores, is the biggest in northwest Mexico.

Rosarito

Thirty minutes' drive farther south, past half a dozen oceanside communities, lies **Rosarito**. Take the toll road on which the traffic is invariably light. South of town the attention of passing motorists is always caught by the sight of the

Above: Tijuana is the place to find painted donkeys
Left: outside the Jai Alai Fronton

almost full-size model of the SS *Titanic*, which was used in the hit movie filmed at the new Fox Studios. Of the several hotels in this little town, the most illustrious is the **Rosarito Beach Hotel** (tel: 800-343-8582), which attracted the early Hollywood crowd. Its glory days are past but it's still worth seeing for the murals by Matias Sontoyo, a huge swimming pool, and Friday and Saturday night dinner shows. South-of-the-border shopping bargains can be found at **Festival Plaza** hotel and mall. Watch out for 'stop' signs at almost every block. You don't want to fall foul of the local police, who might relish the opportunity to stop a law-breaking gringo.

3. San Diego Wild Animal Park *(see map, p48)*

Visit one of the star attractions of the region.

The San Diego Wild Animal Park, in which more than 2,500 creatures roam freely over 2,100 landscaped acres (850ha), is a two to three hours drive north-east of San Diego. Take SR 163 from Balboa Park and stay on it until it segues into I-15, exiting at Via Rancho Parkway. Then follow the signs along SR 78. Alternatively, in San Diego, take I-8 from Ocean Beach and turn northward either on SR 163 or on I-15. (Continuing east on I-8 past San Diego State University leads to the city of La Mesa, an affluent enclave with a spectacular view from the top of Mount Helix). You might want to stop off at the **Mission Basilica San Diego de Alcala** *(see page 37)* en route.

East of I-15, before Escondido, is **Poway**, whose Visitors Center (tel: 619-748-0016) is on the lake. Formerly a stagecoach stop, Poway has century-old buildings, a gazebo, a restaurant, and walking trails. The nearby Blue Sky Ecological Preserve is a canyon whose wildlife is disturbed only by hikers, cyclists, and horseback riders.

The nicest thing about the **San Diego Wild Animal Park** (daily 9am–4pm, later in summer; tel: 760-747-8702) near Escondido is that the animals have so much space in which to roam. This includes a series of interconnected valleys with lakes, pools, rocky cliffs, and sandy desert. Only fences (and occasional moats) keep the different species in their own vast areas. To enjoy the park fully, take the hour-long Wgasa Bush Line monorail ride, during which you'll probably see elephants using their trunks to spray their backs with sand (to keep off the sun); bison standing motionless in ponds; hippos basking in the mud; gazelles, impala and the like herding their young off-spring; and sure-footed goats leaping from crag to crag. You'll also be able to admire ostriches and herds of zebras and giraffes before the chatty guide/driver draws your attention to a group of okapi – 'they look as though they're been put together with spare animal parts.'

Above: zebras enjoy the wild animal park's wide-open spaces

to admire ostriches and herds of zebras and giraffes before the chatty guide/driver draws your attention to a group of okapi – 'they look as though they're been put together with spare animal parts.'

The park, which is run by the San Diego Zoo, prides itself on being a sanctuary for endangered species, 41 of which have been reproduced in the grounds. The latest such success are the rare birds preserved and displayed on Condor Ridge, which also shelters falcons and hawks, and parrots, ferrets, prairie dogs, and bighorn sheep in a pine, spruce, fir, and redwood forest.

The California condor, with a wingspan of up to 10ft (3m), was almost extinct a few years ago, at which time the last surviving wild birds were taken into custody. Since then, the park has bred at least 70 of them. If you are interested in becoming a member of the park, inducements include sleepovers in tents at Kilma Ridge overlooking the East Africa enclosure (you can wake up to the roars of lions and tigers) and subscriptions to the excellent *Zoo News*. Elephants appear in daily animal shows at the amphitheater, there are bird shows, and also a winding walking trail through forest, savannah, and wetlands known as the Heart of Africa exhibit. Photographers might want to reserve a place on one of the 'photo caravans' – open trucks that give camera-toting visitors the opportunity to catch some animal close-ups.

Reliving the Mexican War

On a hillside adjoining SR 78, the **San Pasquale Battlefield State Historic Park** (Sat, Sun 10am–5pm; tel: 760-737-2201) replicates a significant 1846 battle of the Mexican war. Get a pamphlet at the visitors center. If possible you should visit on the first Sunday of the month (Oct–June) when volunteers in period costume reenact battle scenes. Continuing in an eastward direction, SR 78 winds for nearly 36 miles (60km) through mostly deserted countryside. Drive through sleepy little Ramona and the even smaller Santa Ysabel, where you can visit a mission founded in 1818.

The San Pasquale Valley is wine country. Three small vineyards welcome visitors for tastings: the **Orfilia Vineyards** (daily 10am–6pm; tel: 760-738-6500); the **Bernardo Winery** (daily 9am–5pm; tel: 858-487-1866); and also the **Ferrara Winery** (daily 10am–5pm; tel: 760-745-7632).

Seven miles (11km) north of Escondido adjoining the I-15, the **Lawrence Welk Museum** (daily 10am–5pm; tel: 760-749-3448) exhibits memorabilia – such as old photographs, gold records, a giant champagne glass – of the

Above and Right: in the Wild Animal Park.
Far Right: in Julian the west still looks wild

SR S6 from Escondido leads to the 6,000-ft (1,850-m) high Palomar Mountain. Perched on one of the mountain ridges is the **Palomar Observatory** (daily 9am–4pm; tel: 760-7452-2119). From 1948 until the 1970s, its 525-ton Hale Telescope, which has a 200 in (500cm), reflector was the world's largest. Sitting under an Art Deco-style dome seven stories high, it has a mirror made from a 14.5-ton piece of Pyrex, the heaviest piece of glass in the world.

The state park in which the observatory is situated offers pleasant picnic areas and camping facilities.

4. Julian *(see map, p48)*

This historic gold-mining town offers a taste of pioneer life.

About an hour's drive east of the Wild Animal Park along SR 78 is the former gold-mining town of Julian, better known today for its apple pies, cattle ranches, and springtime displays of lilacs and wildflowers. The main street, which hasn't changed much in a century, has a number of bakeries all claiming to sell the best apple pies in town, and the drugstore sports an old-fashioned, marble-topped soda fountain. The white **Wilcox Building** on Main Street was built in 1872 by Horace Fenton Wilcox to house his grocery and hardware store. He built a toll road to connect the gold mines in Julian with others 4 miles (6km) down the canyon in Banner, as well as wagons to carry the ore to San Diego. When he sold the Wilcox building on his retirement in 1897, his successors advertised 'first-class goods at reasonable prices and square dealing with politeness thrown in.'

In the next block the Julian Hotel has been in business since 1897. The original Julian Hotel burned down a century ago on the site of what is today the Town Hall. Around the corner on 4th Street, the **Julian Pioneer Museum** (summer: Tues–Sun 10am–4pm; winter: Sat, Sun only; tel: 760-765-0227) is a typical smalltown wonderland of Native American artifacts, stuffed birds, and Victorian-era curios.

Julian was founded by Drury Robbins Bailey, who homesteaded with his brothers. He named the town, which he also laid out, for his cousin Mike Julian because, he explained, 'Mike was the best looking.' All had been

Confederate soldiers together in Georgia and were seeking a new start in the West. Whereas Mike Julian was appointed county assessor, Drue Bailey benefited from a large stroke of luck. He was virtually broke when he struck gold at a mine he called the Ready Relief. Gold was relatively easy to mine with a pickaxe hereabouts, following the miners' old adage: 'Where there are trees the ground is soft; where there are no trees we have to blast.' At the end of C Street, you can take an hour-long tour in the hillside tunnels of an old mine dug by the **Eagle Mining Company** (daily 10am–3pm; tel: 760-765-0036), which operated until 1942. San Diego County's mines yielded more than $10 million worth of gold by the end of the 19th century.

An Odd Duel

As in any mining town there was considerable rowdiness and many a drunk ended up in the concrete, two-cell **Old Jail**, which can be inspected at 4th and C streets. Prisoners held here were served home-cooked meals by the sheriff's wife. Occasionally the bar-room fights took a more serious turn and on one occasion, when a pair of feuding miners each boasted that they'd kill the other if only they had a gun, Bailey persuaded them to move to an adjoining field to 'shoot it out like men and be done with it.'

Handing pistols to both of the now apprehensive participants, he ordered that they start shooting on a count of three and keep at it till one or the other was dead. After several shots it became apparent that Drue had loaded the guns with blanks. The two miners shook hands and became the best of friends. Bailey's home can be seen on Farmers Road (the western extension of Main Street) and his grave is in the local Haven of Rest Cemetery.

The gold-mining boom lasted through the 1870s, by which time some unsuccessful prospectors, realizing that the climate and terrain were well-suited for growing apples and pears, had turned to farming. One of the first orchards was planted by Chester Gunn who, while still in his 20s, had run

Above: 19th-century stores in Julian sold 'first-class goods with politeness thrown in'

a Pony Express mail service (10 cents a letter) following old Indian trails between Julian and San Diego. The advent of the stagecoach put him out of business and he went on to become Julian's first postmaster.

Entrepreneurs competed to provide the stagecoach route. The San Diego *Daily World* described a ride on July 28, 1872: 'Soon the Mail Stage with two or three passengers and Stokes himself for driver came thundering alongside the Pioneer and made a splendid effort to pass. All was now excitement, drivers, horses and passengers, all anxious to run… The wheels whizzed, the horses' feet clattering, drivers cracked their whips and lashed their panting, foaming coursers, clouds of dust filled the air and the excited passengers joined in the general din and made the confusion worse confounded.' During one battle for customers, passengers on the new line could travel the 60 miles (97km) from San Diego to Julian free. In response the old line offered passengers $1 each to take the trip. This was more than matched by the new line, which offered $1 plus free drinks. The old line soon went out of business.

A pleasant way to get around town is in one of the horse-drawn vehicles of **Country Carriages** (Mon–Fri 11am–4pm, Sat, Sun 11am–9pm; tel: 760-765-1471) from the corner of Main and Washington streets.

Apple Days

Julian has some attractive bed and breakfast accommodations and those staying on Friday or Saturday nights might want to visit the **Pine Hills Lodge and Dinner Theater** (tel: 760-765-1100) just outside town, which lays on a barbecue dinner before the 8pm performance of a play. During the Apple Days celebration after harvest in the fall, the Old-Time Melodrama and Olio is staged (for details call the Chamber of Commerce, tel: 760-765-1857).

State Highways 79 (north to south) and 78 (east to west) intersect at Julian and there are worthwhile attractions on both. On Saturday afternoons the **California Wolf Center** (tel: 760-765-0030) on SR 79 presents an educational program about wolves. The weekend is also the time to visit **Observer's Inn** (tel: 760-765-0088), a commercially run observatory staffed by professional astronomers who will guide you through the mysteries of the firmament. On SR 78, the **Farmers Mountain Vale Ranch** (Sept–May, Mon–Fri 9am–5pm; tel: 760-765-0188) presents lots of farm animals and birds, a rose garden, and free samples of cider.

Three miles (5km) north of Julian, the **Menghini Winery** (daily, summer: 10am–5pm; winter: 10am–4pm; tel: 760/765-2072) welcomes picnickers to its vineyards and apple orchards. There's wine tasting every day and two special events in September: the Grape Stomp Fiesta and the Arts and Music Festival.

Above: commemorating the gold rush. **Right:** easy rider

5. TEMECULA *(see map below)*

Explore California's southernmost wine region.

After a stayover in Julian, Los Angeles-bound travelers might want to make a stop at Temecula, which is on I-15 about 40 miles (65km) north of Escondido. Temecula is the center of a winery district that bears the distinction of being California's southernmost appellation. The area's wine potential was discovered by Jean-Louis Vignes in the 1840s but it was not until the 1960s, that a group of researchers from the University of California at Davis brought Temecula to the attention of the wine-making community.

In the 1850s, Butterfield Overland Mail stagecoaches bustled through what is now the **Old Town Preservation District**. Today the district has antique shops, a courtyard café and Hollywood Souvenirs where you can have your photo taken beside cut-outs of John Wayne or Charlie Chaplin.

Five blocks to the north near the intersection of I-15 and Rancho California Road is **Sam Hicks Park**, named for the historian who served as constable of the region. Hicks first arrived in the valley in 1940 with the mystery writer Erle Stanley Gardner, who created TV's Perry Mason. Hicks managed the famous Rancho del Paisano, which Gardner called his 'fiction factory.'

They Passed This Way

An accomplished writer himself, Hicks spearheaded the drive to commemorate Temecula's pioneers with the monument that sits in this park. The stone marker is named 'They Passed This Way'; 'they' included mountain man Jedediah Smith; Indian scout Kit Carson, who in 1848 was on his way east to spread the word about the gold finds in California; and Helen Hunt Jackson, the author of *Ramona*. This novel about a half-Native American girl adopted by Spanish Californian grandees before being overwhelmed by a tragic destiny has been through 141 editions since 1883.

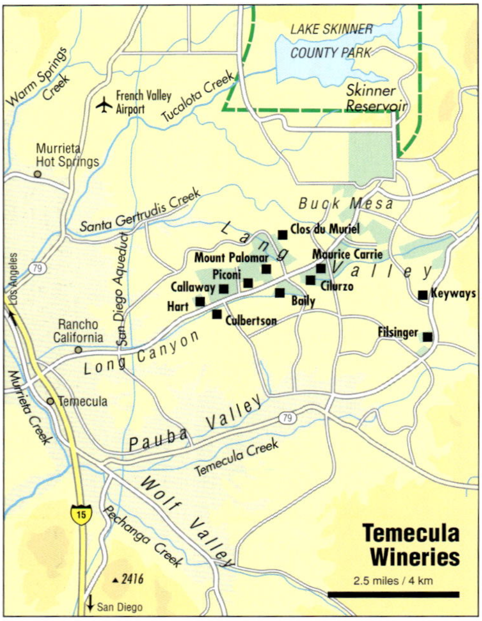

Along Rancho California Road west of Margarita, the **Hart Winery** (daily 9am–4.30pm; tel: 909-676-6300), is the first of nine such wineries along this stretch of highway. Next is the **Callaway Vineyard and Winery** (daily 10:30am–4.45pm; tel: 676-4001) owned by Canadian distillers, Hiram Walker, and across the street, **Thornton** (daily 11am–5pm; tel: 699-0099), whose Café Champagne gourmet eatery uses herbs from its own garden.

Next, on opposite sides of the highway, are the attractive **Mount Palomar** (daily, winter: 10am–5pm; summer: 10am–6pm; tel: 676-5047) owned by media mogul John

Poole, and **Baily** (daily 10am–5pm). Carol and Phil Baily also own **Falkner Winery** (daily 10am–5pm; tel: 676-8231) which, located at the top of the hill, has a fine view of California's five highest peaks. You can sample the wine from lovely glasses bearing a distinctive blue stripe. Most of the winery's production is sold on the premises. **Maurice Carrie Vineyard and Winery** (daily 10am–5pm; tel: 676-1711)) is owned by the Van Roekels. When they bought Cleo Vineyards with its vintage barn and windmill (which appears on labels), they added the winery, for which they adapted the style of a Victorian farmhouse, and planted a veritable profusion of flowers.

Van Roekel Vineyards and Winery (daily 10am–5pm; tel: 699-6961) was acquired when the abandoned winery next door came up for sale and was destined to become a minimart. The oldest of the current crop of wineries, **Cilurzo** (daily 9.30am–5pm; tel: 676-5250) was built on the last of the area's working cattle ranches by Vincenzo and Audrey Cilurzo in 1968 when Temecula's population was less than 200. (Now 31,000 it's one of the state's fastest-growing towns, with 19 million people within a two-hour drive). On nearby De Portola Road are **Filsinger** (Sat, Sun 10.30am–5pm; tel: 676-4594) and **Keyways** (daily 10am–5pm; tel: 676-2532).

During the first weekend in March and the third weekend in November, the wineries collaborate in a food-and-wine festival for which tickets must be obtained in advance. Call any of the aforementioned wineries for details. Like many of the winery stores elsewhere in California, Temecula shops sell a variety of T-shirts, picnic baskets and fancy glasses, but one item is unique: napkins inscribed with the slogan, 'We Don't Care How You Do It Up North.'

The temperate climate enjoyed by the vineyards off Temecula's Rancho California Road comes from a gorge, Rainbow Gap, whose air cools the vineyards at the same time every day. The surrounding mountains are, at between 4,000ft (1,200m) and 6,000ft (1,800m), even higher than those around Napa and Sonoma. 'For every 1,000ft (304m) of altitude,' explains Callaway Vineyards winemaker Dwayne Helmuth, 'the temperature drops three degrees,' making this an ideal spot for growing grapes.

Above: Temecula is vineyard country

6. Anza Borrego Desert (see map, p48)

Experience the natural attractions of this vast State Park.

Eastward from Julian on SR 78 is the huge Anza-Borrego Desert State Park, the largest in the continental US. It is described by a guide as 'a zoo-like mélange of flora and fauna, hikers and cyclists, flowering cacti, palm groves, bighorn sheep, and exotic birds.' In the 1850s the Butterfield Overland Stage traveled through **Borrego Springs** town. The stage route is marked on County Highway S-2, on which two of the stops still stand. The Butterfield left St Louis and Memphis every Monday and Thursday, taking a southerly route over the plains of Texas then crossing the arid lands of New Mexico to enter California near Fort Yuma on the Colorado River.

'A good lookout should be kept for Indians,' wrote a stagecoach veteran. 'No intercourse should be had with them, but let them alone; by no means wrong them. At all times an efficient guard should be kept, and such guard should always be ready for any emergency.'

Stop at the park's **Visitors Center** (winter: daily 9am–5pm; summer: Sat, Sun 9am–5pm; tel: 769/767-5311) for information, and be aware also that midsummer temperatures habitually reach 105°F (40°C) and even in fall are likely to be in the upper 80s (low 30s°C). Near the Visitors Center **Palm Canyon** has an attractive campground where park rangers organize nature walks. Wild flowers are especially lovely in the spring – call the Wildflower Hotline (tel: 760-767-4684) for details. The California Park Service newspaper says that the 2,000 animal species in the park's 781 sq miles (2,000 sq km), 'slither, creep, scamper, flutter, soar, gallop, swim, hop, and prowl among a thousand varieties of prickly, fragrant, oily, pungent, sticky, fuzzy, awe-inspiring flora.'

Frogs and Fish

The creatures vary in size from the cowbird and the tiny pipistrelle bat to bulky bighorn sheep. The not-so-barren desert also shelters frogs and fish, notably the 2in (5cm) pupfish that survives in water saltier than that in the ocean and varying in temperature from 33°F to 108°F (1°C–42°C). The frogs were originally brought by miners to sell to restaurants.

The park is home to 21 different species of bat, which rangers explain are now endangered because so many of their natural habitats are being destroyed. Farmers are the bats' biggest supporters because, in eating harmful insects and moths, they do a great deal to protect crops. The park has numerous well-marked trails and it is one of the few places in the country where open camping is permitted, although a $5 (overnight) or $10 (weekend) permit must be obtained.

Above: taking it easy in the Anza-Borrego Desert State Park

7. San Juan Capistrano *(see map, p48)*

Combine a visit to this mission with a look at Camp Pendleton, the world's largest Marine Corps base.

North of Oceanside, **Camp Pendleton** sprawls over several thousand acres. Camp Pendleton is open to visits by members of the public on most days of the year. Of special interest is the Command Museum (Tues–Sat 10am–4pm, Sun 10am–5pm; tel: 725-5566), which regularly screens a 20-minute film about the Marine Corps. Past the huge, oceanside nuclear power structures at San Onofre is San Clemente, where the **Richard Nixon Library and Birthplace** (daily 10am–5pm, Sun 11am–5pm; tel: 714/993-3393) presents highlights of the former president's life in 22 fully filled rooms. On the grounds is the house in which Nixon was born on January 9, 1913, and nearby is the grave of the president and his wife.

The Mystery of the Swallows

A few miles to the north is the turnoff on SR 74 to **San Juan Capistrano**. Founded by Father Junipero Serra in 1776 as the seventh of the state's coastal missions, it is known for the swallows that return here with a certain amount of predictability on or around March 19, St Joseph's Day, every year. They have been observed leaving Goya in Argentina in late February and their passage tracked through the river valleys of Panama and Paraguay before turning east to bypass the Andes. At altitudes above 2,000ft (620m) they avoid predatory birds and are helped by fast air currents and tailwinds. They have been arriving at Capistrano for centuries but nobody knows why. In recent years, despite the release of ladybugs, a favored food, they have dismayed mission denizens by forsaking the hallowed buildings in favor of the eaves of the local Wal-Mart and Saddleback College.

Cliff swallows, identified by a white forehead, a rust-colored patch at the rear and a very square tail, feed on the wing, catching insects in their beaks, touching the ground so rarely they are barely able to walk. They seek out fresh water and mud as materials with which to build their nests, returning to them year after year following a 7,500 mile (12,000km) flight via Yucatan and the Gulf of Mexico.

A statue of Fr Serra stands beside the ruined **Great Stone Church** to the right as you enter the mission. The Serra chapel, dedicated in 1778, is behind the church and is the oldest building in the state still used for its original purpose. As you enter, pick up a free map of the mission. Not that you need it to find the most interesting structures, the tanning vats, metal furnaces, and tallow ovens, which can be identified in the far-left corner. The gardens were added in the 20th century but the main courtyard looks much as it did when it was the site of rodeos. The 10-acre (4-ha) site has a museum, living quarters for the padres, a kitchen, and gardens. Near the mission are several adobe buildings, two dating to 1794, and the old Santa Fe Railroad depot, built in 1894 Mission Revival style.

Right: something for roller-skating cowboys

Leisure Activities

SHOPPING

Exciting shop-portunities abound in sunny San Diego. Throughout the city you will find beautiful, labyrinthine outdoor mega-malls which are great fun to explore while you pass familiar retail names along the way.

In addition to the chain stores' predictable stucco monoliths are rows of boutiques full of fascinating gear, galleries, antique stores and one-of-a-kind shops. These, the places to go for unique mementos of your travels to this beachfront paradise, are the real finds. The following are some of the best shopping areas in the different regions, each with a special appeal and character all its own.

Most stores, especially those in the shopping centers, are open Mon–Sat 10am–9pm and Sun 11am–7pm. Smaller stores outside the malls tend to close a bit earlier, at around 6 or 7pm. Many of the drugstores, groceries and convenience stores dotted around the city open 24 hours a day, seven days a week.

Downtown/Gaslamp Quarter

A remarkable renaissance has been taking place in downtown San Diego for the past 15 years. One by one, abandoned and decrepit historical buildings have been lovingly restored to their original architectural glory. The revitalization of the city center – with its influx of fashionable boutiques, fine dining, and entertainment venues, along with work/living loft spaces – was initiated by the 1985 opening of Westfield Shoppingtown Horton Plaza, covering seven blocks of a once blighted neighborhood. This should be one of your first stops.

Horton Plaza, designed by the architect Jon Jerde *(see Itinerary 1, page 24)* is considered by many to be an architectural masterpiece. With its whimsical, multilevel design and kaleidoscope of colors, it's easy to see why it's considered the Disneyland of San Diego stores. It's fun to simply walk around, admire the fanciful store facades and peer out over the urban landscape from its many plazas, bridges, and stairways.

The attractive array of 140 establishments includes three major department stores (Macy's, Mervyns, and Nordstrom), a 14-screen movie theater, the Lyceum (home of the San Diego Repertory Theatre), and Planet Hollywood, which has brought some razzmatazz to the north side of the mall, overlooking Horton Park and Broadway.

Not long after Horton Plaza opened, the adjacent historic Gaslamp Quarter embarked on program of slow and steady urban renewal, eventually spreading over 16 blocks. Along Fourth and Fifth avenues, grand Victorian-era buildings have become home to a wide assortment of stores catering to the hip and trendy. Sprinkled between the popular bars and restaurants are art galleries, designer and vintage clothing shops, antique stores, cigar shops, wine sellers and exotic home-decor stores.

Seaport Village, on San Diego Bay next to the Hyatt Regency, is a quaint Victorian-style collection of 75 specialty shops. With such a wide selection of wares, including beachwear, kites, hammocks, and the like, you're sure to find the perfect San Diego souvenir. Enjoy live entertainment by street performers in the plazas and along the boardwalk. You can ride on an 1890s Loof Carousel or in a horse-drawn carriage while taking in views of San Diego Bay, the San Diego-Coronado Bridge and also Coronado Island.

Across the street from

Left: cigars for sale in the Gaslamp Quarter
Right: hawking silver in Tijuana

Seaport Village, on W Market Street, is the Olde Cracker Factory Antiques shopping center. This three-floor collection of individually owned stores is filled with antiques and other collectibles.

Little Italy along India and Columbia streets has become a haven for local artists. Wonderful gallery showrooms, art supply stores, photography shops, and home furnishing studios line the streets.

Coronado

Across the Bay from downtown, in the city of Coronado, you will find the Ferry Landing Marketplace. Built on the site of an old ferry jetty, it is easily accessible by water taxis from the ferry dock just north of Seaport Village. Admire the quite beautiful bayfront setting while browsing through the many shops, galleries, restaurants, and cafés. You can also rent a cycle from here to explore other scenic sights on the island, whose grande dame is undoubtedly the splendidly Victorian Hotel del Coronado.

Hillcrest/Uptown

Uptown's Hillcrest neighborhood represents the funkier, alternative side of San Diego shopping. Fifth and University avenues are lined with antique and thrift stores, record shops, second-hand bookstores, a Gothic candle shop, flower and garden stands, kitschy novelty shops, a piercing studio, adult video stores, newsstands, bakeries, organic grocery stores, and disco-clothing boutiques. Hillcrest is so hip that even one of corporate America's biggest names has discovered its allure and set up shop on one prominent street corner (hint: it starts with a G and rhymes with map).

The city's new bohemians have also been known to frequent the eclectic collection of antique stores and New Age shops along Adams Avenue in University Heights and Kensington. Mission Hills, with its French-style boutiques and salons around Goldfinch and Washington streets, is another characterful neighborhood worth exploring.

Old Town

Old Town, the birthplace of California, is a region steeped in history. Many of the city's original buildings (some made of adobe) still stand and are home to little shops selling imported Mexican items; colorful reminders of just how close San Diego is to Mexico both geographically and culturally.

Be sure to check out Bazaar del Mundo,

Above: a Tijuana market stall
Left: some like it hot

a festive cosmopolitan marketplace in Old Town State Park that's home to enchanting ethnic arts and crafts shops, splashing fountains, fun-filled dining patios, strolling mariachis, and swirling folkloric dancers.

Mission Valley

Just northeast of Old Town, Mission Valley offers more contemporary retailing options. The valley is anchored by two large outdoor shopping centers. Westfield Shoppingtown Mission Valley is a sprawling vibrant venue encompassing 100 specialty stores, the department stores Robinsons-May, Wards and Nordstrom Rack, and AMC 20 Theatres. The two-story Fashion Valley Center has some 200 exclusive stores and six large department stores: Neiman-Marcus, Macy's, Nordstrom, Robinsons-May, JC Penney, and Saks Fifth Avenue. As the name implies, it's somewhat more fashionable than its sister center down the road; in fact it's a grand outdoor monument to upscale mall shopping.

La Jolla

Prospect Street in La Jolla village is more enticing and seductive than Rodeo Drive in Beverly Hills dut to its seafront setting – white sand coves and clear blue waters are a few steps away. Some of San Diego's finest art galleries – specializing in antiquities, photos, contemporary art, animation, glass works, early Californian paintings, sculpture, and drawings – are here. As impressive are the boulevards of fashion boutiques, florists, jewelers, salons, and bookstores.

Farther inland, Westfield Shoppingtown University Towne Centre in the Golden Triangle offers a park-like, outdoor shopping center experience. UTC, as it's known, has 155 stores, including department-store outlets Nordstrom, Sears, Robinsons-May and Macy's, and an Olympic-size ice skating rink for some much needed relief from the heat.

Del Mar

A short leisurely stroll from the surf and sand, on Camino del Mar, is Del Mar Plaza. Indulgent shopping delights here range from locally inspired fine arts to assorted jewelry and contemporary designer apparel. After a lazy afternoon of shopping, you could relax in one of the big deck chairs that overlook the Pacific. They say that life doesn't get any better than this, and they're not wrong.

Solana Beach

Locals flock to S Cedros Avenue in Solana Beach (just north of Del Mar and just east of Pacific Coast Highway) to browse through the artist/interior design studios, flower-design shops and furniture/home decor emporiums. You could conceivably furnish your entire home with the classic, fantastic, exotic, and magical creations on display here.

Outlet Shopping

Outlet shopping is popular throughout San Diego, whose three major outlet malls beckon brand-name bargain hunters. Just off I-5 near Legoland, the Carlsbad Company Stores has more than 70 well-known designer and manufacturer names. The wonderful winery and some restaurants are likely to tempt your taste buds.

In the South Bay city of San Ysidro on the Mexican border, the San Diego Factory Outlet Center has 35 factory stores – the treasures of Tijuana are only a short walk away.

Viejas Outlet Center is a discount oasis in the hills of San Diego's East County on the Viejas Indian reservation in Alpine. The rustic southwestern architecture is a marvel in itself. You could easily forget that you're surrounded by 36 big-name stores, as you walk beside splashing streams. The nightly laser-light and music show is a big draw.

Above: the rainbow colors of Tijuana beadwork

EATING OUT

With more than 6,400 restaurants, San Diego is a diner's delight. Locals enjoy an eclectic mix of culinary offerings inspired by the region's Mediterranean climate, fresh and plentiful produce, health-conscious lifestyle, and rich blend of cultures, most notably those from Mexico and the Pacific Rim. Signature regional dishes range from zesty, authentic Mexican food and Asian-fusion creations to lighter California cuisine. With its 70 miles (110km) of pristine beaches hugging the ocean, it's easy to see why the city is also synonymous with savory seafood platters.

The city's dining scene is becoming one of the hottest in the nation, thanks, in part, to the dynamic revitalization of its downtown historic district, the Gaslamp Quarter. In recent years, the Gaslamp has become *the* place to wine and dine, especially in the evenings and on weekends. The Gaslamp's bustling main thoroughfares, Fourth and Fifth avenues, now house over 80 eateries.

A number of the city's neighborhoods and suburbs are known for their tantalizing, mouth-watering array of bistros: downtown's Little Italy is a characterful village of Italian eateries and bakeries; Hillcrest is uptown's hip and happening dining spot, whereas Mission Hills is uptown's more relaxed dining hideaway; Old Town is the birthplace of San Diego Mexican cuisine; and La Jolla, San Diego's Riviera, offers some of the finest dining establishments.

San Diego County is an enormous, diverse region, with a number of cities and towns spread out along the coast, in the foothills and mountains, and in the deserts. Wherever you go, a banquet of fine cuisine awaits. The following are some of the best known and loved restaurants and cafés.

$ = up to $10 per person
$$ = $10–$20
$$$ = $20 plus

Anthony's Star of the Sea
1360 Harbor Drive
(Downtown)
Tel: (619) 232-7408.
The pearl of local seafood restaurants, Anthony's Star of the Sea presents coastal cuisine in a contemporary – and romantic – setting right on the water; spectacular views of San Diego Bay. **$$$**

Athens Market Taverna
109 W F Street
(Downtown)
Tel: (619) 234-1955.
A very popular choice with the locals, Athens Market Taverna is an upscale, award-winning Greek restaurant located right next to the Horton Plaza. **$$**

Bandar
825 4th Avenue
(Gaslamp Quarter)
Tel: (619) 238-0101.
Fine Persian cuisine in a contemporary setting. Entrees are bold and flavorful. **$$**

Bayou Bar & Grill
329 Market Street
(Gaslamp Quarter)
Tel: (619) 696-8747.
Delicious Cajun/Creole creations in a casual dining environment. **$$**

Above: take a break from the heat in an ice cream parlor in Tijuana
Right: fun is on the menu at the Horton Plaza shopping center

Bertrand at Mister A's
2550 Fifth Avenue
(Bankers Hill)
Tel: (619) 239-1377.
Bertrand at Mister A's is a legendary rooftop restaurant that features modern American cuisine along with bird's-eye views of the city and the bay. **$$**

Big Kitchen
3003 Grape Street
(Golden Hill)
Tel: (619) 234-5789.
Casual home-style dining. Try the 'Whoopi Goldberg' – two eggs, four rashers of bacon and grilled potatoes – which is named for the *Sister Act* star who waitressed here for a short time before making her name as a comedy actress in Hollywood. **$**

Bob's on the Bay
570 Marina Parkway
(Chula Vista)
Tel: (619) 476-0400.
Spacious patio overlooks the marina. Freshly caught fish is a specialty. Try the papiotte mahi-mahi wrapped in parchment. **$$**

Cafe 222
222 Island Avenue
(Downtown)
Tel: (619) 236-9902.
This hip urban coffee shop/bistro is renowned for its distinctive and eclectic menus – breakfast features such unusual fare as pumpkin waffles; for lunch you could try the salmon burgers. **$**

Café on Park
3831 Park Boulevard
(Hillcrest)
Tel: (619) 293-7275.
With hearty breakfasts and large lunches complementing a chic industrial interior, it's no wonder that Café on Park is so popular, especially on weekends. **$$**

Café Japengo
8960 University Center Lane
Tel: (858) 450-3355.
Progressive Pacific Rim dishes and sushi delicacies in a sleek, Far East setting attract a fashionable crowd. **$$**

Casa de Bandini-Bazaar del Mundo
2660 Calhoun Street
(Old Town)
Tel: (619) 297-8211.
Mexican eatery in a historic hacienda, great for margaritas and mariachis. **$**

Chez Loma French Bistro
1132 Loma Avenue
Coronado
Tel: (619) 435-0661.
Located in a Victorian house, Chez Loma rates high on the quaint scale and features an acclaimed French dinner menu. **$$**

Chive
558 Fourth Avenue
(Gaslamp Quarter)
Tel: (619) 232-4483.
Stunning new eatery with sophisticated menu catering for modern clientele. **$$$**

The Corvette Diner
3946 Fifth Avenue
(Hillcrest)
Tel: (619) 542-1001.
This good old-fashioned, 1950s-style diner is dedicated to rock 'n' roll. Dancing in the aisles is encouraged. **$**

Crest Café
425 Robinson Avenue
(Hillcrest)
Tel: (619) 295-2510.
A cozy, casual neighborhood bistro that serves hearty, healthy American fare. Open till midnight. **$**

Dine with Shamu
Sea World
(Mission Bay)
Tel: (619) 226-3601.
Outdoor dining area beside Shamu's private pool. The expensive buffet menu carries the warning: 'whales may splash during your Shamu experience.' **$$$**

El Indio
3695 India Street
(Mission Hills)
(also downtown, 409 F Street)
Tel: (619) 299-0333.
A San Diego institution, El Indio has been serving Mexican food since the 1940; tasty taquitos, homemade tortillas. **$**

El Zarape Mexican Restaurant
4642 Park Boulevard
(University Heights)
Tel: (619) 692-1652.
El Zarape is a tiny cantina (tavern) that has not received the recognition it deserves for its delicious Mexican seafood. **$**

Fio's Cucina Italiana
801 Fifth Avenue
(Gaslamp Quarter)
Tel: (619) 234-3467.
Fio's Cucina Italiana is justifiably one of the most recognizable names in the downtown area. Famous for its award-winning northern Italian cuisine. **$$$**

George's at the Cove
1250 Prospect Street
(La Jolla)
Tel: (858) 454-4244.
The seafood at George's is as sensational as the views of La Jolla Cove. For more casual dining, try the Ocean Terrace. **$$-$$$**

Filippi's Pizza Grotto
1747 India Street
(Little Italy and six other locations)
Filippi's home-style pizzas have become a San Diego tradition. This Italian-style chain features fun settings and old-fashioned decor, right down to the traditional red and white checkered tablecloths. **$**

Above: a San Diego soda fountain tops the bill

Kansas City Barbecue
610 W Market Street
(Downtown)
Tel: (619) 231-9680.
This casual dive, which became famous with its appearance in the movie *Top Gun*, is a local favorite for its wonderfully messy, finger-licking barbecue specialties. **$**

Karl Strauss Brewery and Restaurant
1157 Columbia Street
(Downtown)
Tel: (619) 234-BREW.
(other locations in Sorrento Mesa, La Jolla and Carlsbad)
San Diego's original and best microbrewery restaurant chain is known not only for its handcrafted beers but also for its excellent American-grill cuisine. **$**

Kemo Sabe
3958 Fifth Avenue
(Hillcrest)
Tel: (619) 220-6802.
The presentation is as good as the Pacific Rim cuisine at this fine uptown restaurant. Kemo Sabe's glossy, southwestern-style interior is complemented by entrees that are zesty, colorful works of culinary art. **$$**

Marine Room
2000 Spindrift Drive
(La Jolla)
Tel: (858) 459-7222.
The Marine Room presents seafront dining at its best. Award-winning haute cuisine and dramatic ocean views. The waves come crashing right up against the windows. **$$**

Mille Fleurs
6009 Paseo Delicias Rancho Santa Fe
Tel: (858) 756-3085.
An elegant, romantic restaurant, Mille Fleurs specializes in French cuisine. Good for serial diners as the menu changes every day. **$$**

Mimmo's Italian Village
1743 India Street
(Little Italy)
Tel: (619) 233-3237.
Locals flock to Mimmo's, especially for lunch, for the deli-style Italian fare. Both the village-style interior and the sidewalk patio are great for people-watching. **$**

Mixx
3671 Fifth Avenue
(Hillcrest)
Tel: (619) 299-6499.
Mixx's bold approach to dining presents a mouthwatering combination of recipes from virtually every ethnic background. This is a popular choice with the locals so expect large crowds. **$$**

Old Town Mexican Café y Cantina
2489 San Diego Avenue
(Old Town)
Tel: (619) 297-4330.
This is where locals meet for what some claim is the best Mexican food in town. Known for its handmade tortillas. **$**

150 Grand Café
150 W Grand Avenue Escondido
Tel: (760) 738-6868.
One of North County's finest restaurants, 150 Grand Café serves California/Pacific cuisine and exceptional wines. It also features a rotating art gallery. **$$**

Pacifica Del Mar
1555 Camino Del Mar, 321
(Del Mar Plaza)
Tel: (858) 792-0476.
Exceptional coastal cuisine (sample the sugar-spiced salmon) and sweeping vistas of the Pacific. **$$**

Left: Coronado ferry landing restaurant

Parallel 33
741 W Washington Street
(Mission Hills)
Tel: (619) 260-0033.
Uptown eatery that serves sensational foods representing exotic regions on the 33rd parallel (approximately here). **$$**

Peohe's
1201 First Street
(Ferry Landing Marketplace)
Coronado
Tel: (619) 437-4474.
San Diego meets Hawaii in this sensational seafood restaurant on San Diego Bay. Great evening views of the city skyline. **$$$**

Point Loma Seafoods
2805 Emerson Street
Tel: 619) 223-1109.
Forty-year-old family restaurant whose third generation now serves everything from sushi to sandwiches. **$$**

The Prado
1549 El Prado
(Balboa Park)
Tel: (619) 557-9441.
The Prado is one of the park's most fashionable bistros, and is a feast for the senses. The California-southwestern cuisine has a pronounced Mediterranean/Latino twist, and the setting is in the stylish, whimsical surroundings of a Spanish alcazar (castle). **$$**

Rockin' Baja Lobster
258 Harbor Drive South
(Oceanside)
Tel: (760) 967-6199.
Like the eateries on Baja's northern coast, this restaurant serves big buckets of lobster tails, shrimp, and marinated chicken. **$$**

Roppongi
875 Prospect Street
(La Jolla)
Tel: (858) 551-5252.
Asian-fusion – in the bold, tasty cuisine and in the soothing Feng Shui design. **$$$**

Rubios Baja Grill
4504 Mission Bay Drive
(Mission Bay)
Tel: (858) 272-2801.
(25 locations throughout San Diego)
Home of Baja's fish taco. **$**

Saffron
3737 India Street
(Mission Hills)
Tel: (619) 574-7737.
Old-fashioned Thai spicy noodles. **$**

Sammy's Woodfired Pizza
770 Fourth Avenue
(Gaslamp Quarter)
Tel (619) 230-8888.
(five county locations)
Imaginative gourmet pizzas and huge healthy salads draw the crowds. **$$**

Sevilla
555 Fourth Avenue
(Gaslamp Quarter)
Tel: (619) 233-5979.
One of the area's best Spanish restaurants, featuring delicious coastal Spanish cuisine and a festive flamenco dinner show. **$$**

Taste of Thai
527 University Avenue
(Hillcrest)
Tel: (619) 291-7525.
Small uptown favorite that attracts scores of loyal Thai food fans nightly. **$**

Turf Supper Club
1116 25th Street
(Golden Hill)
Tel: (619) 234-6363.
Cook your own kebabs and steaks at this swinging retro-style bar and restaurant. **$$**

Left: the home of Baja's fish taco

NIGHTLIFE

When the sun goes down, San Diego's nightlife starts to crackle and fizz. This is the time when the city's ostensibly laid-back locals display their playful side, especially downtown in the Gaslamp Quarter, the city's prime entertainment area. The streets here are lined with bars and nightclubs catering to almost every musical taste. Weekend nights can be rather crowded, but once you find a parking space (Horton Plaza's parking structure is your best bet), a fun-filled night out on the town awaits.

In communities like Mission Beach and Pacific Beach, the relaxed beach crowd also comes alive when the sun sets. Surfers and the college-age set pack the many bars and clubs along Garnet Avenue and Mission Boulevard most nights.

San Diego bars tend to close at 2am – local laws prohibit bars from serving alcohol past that hour, but a few after-hours clubs stay open until 4am. Certainly by midnight most bars and clubs are in full swing. Conversely, for a more relaxed evening of cultural delights, take in a show at one of the performing arts theaters, which offer Broadway quality (and sometimes Broadway-bound) musicals and plays; world-class opera, and symphony orchestra concerts.

Local rock, jazz, and blues bands can also be found at various venues around town. Multiplex movie theaters present the latest Hollywood blockbusters; Balboa Park is home to the world's first IMAX theater.

Night owls should check out the coffeehouses where you'll find many revelers winding down their evening over a cup of coffee, dessert, and tales of club adventures. The following are local nightlife highlights.

Performing Arts

San Diego features a flourishing visual and performing arts scene. Call (800) 270-WAVE or log onto www.sandiegoartandsol.com to obtain a free colorful brochure, *San Diego Art + Sol*, which spotlights the latest line-up of musicals, theater, dramatic productions, museum exhibits, classical music and more.

Half-price tickets for many theater and performing arts groups are sold on the day of performance at the Times Arts Tix booth, located downtown in Horton Park (next to Horton Plaza) on Broadway Circle, tel: (619) 497-5000.

La Jolla Playhouse
2910 La Jolla Village Drive
La Jolla (UCSD campus)
Tel: (619) 550-1010.
La Jolla Playhouse is a Tony Award-winning theater that frequently presents world premieres, and specializes in musicals, classic dramas and comedies, staged in its two auditoriums.

Above: the Juke Joint Café is the city's jazziest supper club

Lamb's Players Theatre
1142 Orange Avenue
Coronado
Tel: (619) 437-0600.
One of San Diego's leading professional theater groups performs year-round productions in an intimate, European-style theater.

Old Globe Theatre
El Prado, Balboa Park
Tel: (619) 239-2255.
The Tony Award-winning theater graces its three stages, including one outdoors, with top-notch musicals, dramas, and classic Shakespeare productions.

San Diego Civic Theatre
Third and C Street
Tel: (619) 570-1100.
The city's premiere venue is home to the magnificent San Diego Opera and the San Diego Playgoers Series of nationally touring Broadway shows.

San Diego Repertory Theatre
79 Horton Plaza
Tel: (619) 231-3586.
This popular professional theatre group presents six plays annually on its resident stage at the underground Lyceum.

San Diego Symphony Orchestra
Copley Symphony Hall
1245 Seventh Avenue
Tel: (619) 235-0804.
The local Symphony Orchestra presents inspiring classical masterworks throughout the year in one of San Diego's oldest and grandest theaters.

Starlight Musical Theatre
San Diego Civic Light Opera
Starlight Bowl, Balboa Park
Tel: (619) 544-7827.
Broadway-quality musical theater presented under starry skies; a local theater tradition.

Sushi Performance and Visual Art
320 Eleventh Avenue
Tel: (619) 235-8466.
In the artsy East Village, Sushi hosts cutting-edge dance, performance and visual arts.

Movie Theaters

AMC Mission Valley 20
Westfield Shoppingtown Mission Valley Center
1640 Camino del Rio N
Tel: (858) 558-2AMC.

AMC Fashion Valley 18
Fashion Valley Center
7037 Friars Rd
Tel: (858) 558-2AMC.

IMAX Dome
Reuben H. Fleet Science Center
1875 El Prado, Balboa Park
Tel: (619) 238-1233.

Pacific Gaslamp Stadium 15
701 Fifth Avenue
(Gaslamp Quarter)
Tel: (619) 232-0400.
Retro Art Deco movie palace.

UA Horton Plaza Cinema
475 Horton Plaza
Tel: (619) 234-4661.

Bars and Nightclubs

The Alibi
1403 University Avenue
(Hillcrest)
Tel: (619) 295-0881.
At 'Hillcrest's oldest neighborhood bar', an eclectic mix of local hipsters and friendly folks play pool, jam to the jukebox, or just cozy up to the bar.

Barefoot Bar and Grill
San Diego Paradise Point Resort
1404 W Vacation Road
(Mission Bay)
Tel: (858) 274-4630.
Renowned night spot with all-sand dance floor and patio overlooking Mission Bay.

Belly Up Tavern
143 S Cedros Avenue
Solana Beach
Tel: (858) 481-8140.
This converted World War II era Quonset hut books some of the best bands around. Bar, large dance floor and superior sound system.

The Bitter End
770 Fifth Avenue
(Gaslamp Quarter)
Tel: (619) 338-9300.
The place for imaginative martinis (try the Black Martini with Kahlua and chilled espresso). Other fab features: underground dance club, pool, and elegant lounging.

Brick by Brick
1130 Buenos Avenue
Tel: (619) 275-LIVE.
Cozy cocktail tables, a large dance floor and a massive sound system for jamming, live bands or DJs.

Buffalo Joe's Restaurant & Bar
600 Fifth Avenue
(Gaslamp Quarter)
Tel: (619) 236-1616.
Late-night menu and nightly live music with bands playing country, rock 'n' roll, '80s favorites, and 1970s disco.

Cannibal Bar
Catamaran Hotel
3999 Mission Boulevard
(Pacific Beach)
Tel: (858) 539-8651.
Party with some of the best local bands in elegant surroundings.

The Casbah
2501 Kettner Boulevard
Tel: (619) 232-4355.
Small, dark club caters to the numerous local rock bands, their followers, and loud-music aficionados. Features a full bar, dance floor, and an outdoor smoking patio.

Croce's Restaurants and Bars
802 Fifth Avenue
(Gaslamp Quarter)
Tel: (619) 233-4355.
Established as a tribute to Jim Croce, and run by the late musician's wife, the three bars and two restaurants (American cuisine) are landmarks of downtown's nightlife scene. Nightly live jazz and R&B

Dick's Last Resort
345 Fourth Avenue
(Gaslamp Quarter)
Tel: (619) 231-9100.
Rude, crude, and fun. Live music every night.

E Street Alley (Chino)
919 Fourth Avenue
(Gaslamp Quarter)
Tel: (619) 231-9200.
The dressed-to-impress crowd frequents E Street Alley – a basement hideaway that resembles a stylish Prohibition speakeasy. Upscale in-crowd revelers enjoy dancing, pool, and bars.

Left: the Horton Plaza movie theater is itself a work of art
Right: one of numerous live-music options

4th & B
345 B Street
Tel: (619) 231-4343.
Formerly a bank, this concert venue seats crowds of up to 1,500. National touring bands, standup comedians and dance-club acts regularly entertain the masses here.

The Jewel Box
805 16th Avenue
Tel: (619) 236-8685.
This bar's a real dive, but that's what makes it a classic. The clientele's a mix of bikers (a sign out front reads 'Harley Parking Only') and downtown office workers. Play pool or tabletop shuffleboard.

Juke Joint Café
327 Fourth Avenue
(Gaslamp Quarter)
Tel: (619) 232-SOUL.
San Diego's jazziest supper club serves soul food nightly. The back room jumps on weekends with live entertainment.

Lancers Cocktail Lounge
4671 Park Boulevard
(University Heights)
Tel: (619) 298-5382.
This swinging 1960s-era bar attracts lots of young people, as well as middle-aged regulars. You can shoot some pool in the wood-paneled recreation room.

Studio 64 at Club Montage
2028 Hancock Street
Tel: (619) 294-9590.
San Diego's largest dance club arena (three stories) electrifies Friday nights with Studio 64. Fly guys and disco divas pack the place till 4am for high energy dance music.

Olé Madrid
755 Fifth Avenue
Tel: (619) 557-0146.
The evening begins with flamenco dancers and guitarists, whose performances will have you on your feet even if you're in the middle of eating dinner. By mid-evening the place dons a classy disco atmosphere for downtown movers and groovers.

The Onyx Room
852 Fifth Avenue
(Gaslamp Quarter)
Tel: (619) 235-6699.
This popular basement club is a great place to dance to old-school and hip-hop music. Also features a cocktail lounge, piano bar, and live music acts.

Red Fox Room
2223 El Cajon Boulevard
Tel: (619) 297-1313.
This piano-bar is a swanky, leather-seated reminder of how cocktails used to be enjoyed; the ultra-lounge experience. Stand up and sing along with the gruff and sequined old-timers who tickle the ivories.

Club Hedonism at Rich's
1051 University Avenue
(Hillcrest)
Tel: (619) 295-2195.
Every Thursday night enjoy San Diego's ultimate underground club experience. Throngs of friendly disco fans line up round the block for hand-raising hard house and techno tunes.

Top of the Hyatt
Hyatt Regency San Diego
1 Market Place
Tel: (619) 232-1234.
Sip cocktails in style from the 40th floor of the West Coast's tallest waterfront building.

Above: New York isn't the only American city with a hip Fifth Avenue

CALENDAR OF EVENTS

Get a list of the year's activities ($15) from the Visitor Information Center, 11 Horton Plaza, San Diego 92101, tel: (619) 236-1212.

January

New Year's Day Regatta, Shelter Island, tel: (619) 274-9924.
Martin Luther King Jr Day Parade, tel: (619) 264-0542.
San Diego Boat Show, Marriott Hotel Marina, tel: (619) 272-9924.

February

Chinese New Year Food and Cultural Faire, Downtown, tel: (619) 234-4447.
San Diego International Film Festival, UCSD, La Jolla, tel: (858) 534-0497.

March

Classic Festival of Animation, La Jolla, tel: (858) 459-8707.
Mardi Gras in the Gaslamp Quarter, tel: (619) 233-5227.

April

Magnolia Festival of the Arts and Jazz, El Cajon, tel: (619) 440-6161.

May

Wildflower Show, Julian Town Hall, tel: (760) 765-1857.

June

Mainly Mozart Festival, San Diego & Baja, tel: (619) 239-0100.
San Diego Blues Festival, Embarcadero Marina park, tel: (619) 283-9576.
Festival of the Arts and Food Fair, La Jolla, tel: (858) 456-1268.
Scottish Highland Games, Vista, tel: (619) 645-8080.

July

Independence Day celebrations held throughout the nation
Bastille Day Party, French-American Internatonal School, tel: (619) 222-8745.

Right: Hawaiians join the celebrations

US Open Sandcastle Competition, Imperial Beach Pier, tel: (619) 424-6663.

August

World Body Surfing Championships, Oceanside, tel: (760) 966-4536.
Midnight Madness Fun Bicycle Ride, Naval Training Center, tel: (619) 645-8068.

September

Mexican Independence Day Fiesta, Calexico, tel: (760) 357-1166.
Old Town's Fall Fiesta, Mexican Independence Day, tel: (619) 229-5422.
Cabrillo Festival, Cabrillo National Monument, tel: (619) 557-5450.

October

Art, Wine and Culinary Festival, Rancho Bernardo Winery, tel (858) 487-1767.
Zoo Founders Day, free admission to all at San Diego Zoo, tel: (619) 234-3153.
Columbus Day Parade, tel: (619) 469-0795.
Borrego Days Desert Festival, Borrego Springs, tel: (800) 559-5524.

November

Thanksgiving Dixieland Jazz Festival, tel: (619) 297-5277.

December

Christmas on the Prado, Balboa Park, tel: (619) 235-1100.
North Park Toyland Parade, tel: (619) 615-8585.

EAST
SOUTH
CALIFORNIA 78
CALIFORNIA 79
RONG BRANCH RESTAURANT
JULIAN CLOWN SHOP
EAGLENEST B&B
QUINN KNIVES
JULIAN PROPERTIES
HILDRETH HOUSE B&B
BOOK HOUSE
ANGELS LANDING
FALCON GALLERY
BELL BOOK &
HISTORICAL HOUSE B&B
BAILEY'S BARBEQUE
APPLEWOOD HOME DECOR
WINERY
CORNER TO HERE

Practical *Information*

GETTING THERE

By Air

With the ever-growing popularity of the internet, vacation planning and booking of flights has never been simpler or more affordable. Most airlines offer exclusive online airfares. Be sure to contact your local travel agent for additional special deals. Summer is peak season in San Diego, and airfares are generally higher then. In the fall and winter, tourism eases a bit, as do the rates. Whatever the season, look out for unexpected airline 'fare wars.'

San Diego International Airport in Lindbergh Field is one of the most convenient, centrally located airports of any major US city. It is in the heart of downtown, next to towering skyscrapers and San Diego Bay. From the airport, accommodations and most major attractions are just minutes away. Lindbergh Field is served by 16 major airlines.

For details of airport-related services see below or call the general airport information line, tel: (619) 231-2100.

Currency Exchange The Travelex America booth in Terminal 1 is open daily to meet all arriving flights. Information, tel: (619) 295-1501. ATMs are also located in Terminal 1, Terminal 2 and the Commuter Terminal.

Accommodation booking services You can find all levels of accomodations – from basic youth hostels and bed & breakfast motels to luxury, five-star resorts – throughout San Diego and you can make reservations on arrival at the airport at the hotel reservations counters in Terminal 1, Terminal 2 and the Commuter Terminal. Alternately, you can make local reservations by calling San Diego Hotel Reservations, tel: (858) 627-9300.

Shopping Gift shops and newsstands/bookstores can be found primarily in Terminal 2. There are food courts in both Terminal 1 and Terminal 2. Information, tel: (619) 231-5100.

General information To pick up visitor information when you arrive in San Diego visit the Travelers Aid booths in Terminal 1 (tel: 619-231-7361) and on the east and west side of Terminal 2 (tel: 619-231-2278 and 619-231-5230).

By Rail

The main AMTRAK rail line for San Diego is the Pacific Surfliner. It travels north–south, connecting most major cities in central and Southern California, including 11 round-trips per day to Los Angeles. The Santa Fe Depot is San Diego's downtown train station, at 1050 Kettner Boulevard.

For all AMTRAK information, tel: (800)-USA-RAIL. The two-decker Coaster train connects downtown San Diego with the coastal cities of North County. Information, tel: (800)-COASTER.

By Road

You can take one of three major Interstate freeways to San Diego. Interstate 5 (I-5) travels north–south from Canada, via most major cities on the Pacific coast to the border at Tijuana, Mexico. Interstate 15 is also north–south, but is a bit more inland. I-15 begins at the Canadian border in Montana,

Left: a selection of destinations
Right: the boat from Coronado

San Diego's Climate

	Avge Max Temp °F/°C	Avge Min Temp °F/°C	Avge Rain (ins/cm)	% Sun
Jan	65/18	48/9	2.1/5.3	72
Feb	66/19	50/10	1.4/3.6	72
March	66/19	52/11	1.6/4.1	70
April	68/20	55/13	0.8/2	67
May	69/21	58/14	0.2/0.6	59
June	71/22	61/16	0.06/0.2	58
July	76/24	65/18	0.01/0	68
Aug	78/26	67/19	0.1/0.3	70
Sept	77/25	65/18	0.2/0.5	69
Oct	75/24	60/16	0.3/0.8	68
Nov	70/21	54/12	1.1/2.8	75
Dec	66/19	49/10	1.4/3.6	73

Source: National Weather Service

eventually meandering through the foothills of San Diego's North County and ending in downtown San Diego. Interstate 8 travels east–west. Beginning in southern Arizona, it winds through rustic hinterland, arid deserts and pristine mountains, and ends up by the lagoons of Mission Bay.

Driving tip: It is useful to remember that odd-numbered Interstate freeways and state highways travel north– south; even-numbered ones travel east–west.

By Bus

Greyhound, the region's main national bus company, operates 26 daily trips between Los Angeles (which connects with all main US cities) and the San Diego bus terminal at 120 W Broadway; tel: (619) 239-8082 or (800) 231-2222.

By Sea

A number of cruise lines frequent San Diego's perfect natural harbor include Royal Caribbean International, Holland America, Princess, Carnival, Norwegian, Celebrity, Cunard, and Seabourn. These majestic vessels travel from the Caribbean to Mexico and Hawaii, and dock at the B Street Cruise Ship Terminal.

From the Airport

Located on Harbor Drive, just across from Harbor Island, Lindbergh Field can be accessed by car, taxi, shuttle, or city bus.

Taxis

The airport taxi stands are on the street level, outside Terminal 1, Terminal 2 and the Commuter Terminal. Expect to pay $2 for the first mile (1.6km) and $1.40 for every mile thereafter. The fare to most destinations is low, as the airport is already downtown.

Bus

San Diego's city bus The Flyer–Route 992 offers a 10-minute service to and from downtown, connecting with AMTRAK, the Coaster, San Diego trolley, and other bus routes linking the San Diego region. Route 992 stops are just outside Terminal 1, Terminal 2 and the Commuter Terminal. Bus fares are $1–$3. For further information on city buses tel: (800)-COM-MUTE or log on to their website: www.sdcommute.com.

Car Rental

A number of car-rental companies operate just outside Lindbergh Field along Harbor Drive. You can call for courtesy pick-ups at the reservation boards in baggage-claim areas or go directly to the Transportation Plaza outside each terminal and look for

Right: sports fans start young in San Diego

courtesy vans/shuttles. Car rental agencies include the following:

Alamo, tel: (800) 327-9633
Avis, tel: (519) 688-5000
Budget Rent-A-Car, tel: (619) 235-8313
Dollar, tel: (619) 234-3388
Hertz, tel: (619) 220-5222
National, tel: (619) 497-6773
Thrifty, tel: (619) 702-0570

TRAVEL ESSENTIALS

Visas and Passports

Before traveling abroad, it's always a good idea to contact the US embassy in your own country for the latest regulations on visas and passports. Generally, a non-US citizen must present a passport and a valid visa issued by a US consular official.

Weather

San Diego has the US's most moderate Mediterranean climate. The average daily temperature is 70°F (20°C) so pack shorts and swimsuits. February is the coolest month, August the warmest. It can rain in winter, but average annual rainfall is less than 10 in (25cm). Most days are sunny and mild. Evenings are cool; it's always a good idea to carry a light jacket or sweater.

Inland, San Diego's desert temperatures can soar to 100+° in summer. In winter, it can snow in the higher mountain areas above 1,800 meters (6,000ft).

MONEY MATTERS

Currency

United States currency works on the decimal system of dollars and cents (100 cents to the dollar). There are $100, $50, $20, $10, $5, $2 and $1 notes, the recently introduced Sacagawea gold-colored $1 coin and 50, 25, 10, 5 and 1 cent coins. There is no limit on the amount of money (whether it is in the form of coins, currency, travelers' checks or money orders, US or foreign) that may be brought into or taken out of the United States. However, if you want to bring more than $10,000 into or out of the US, you are obliged to complete the relevant US Customs report – form 4790.

Changing Money

Changing foreign currency or travelers' checks is easier at large bank branches. Normal banking hours are Mon–Fri 9am–5pm. Banks are closed on Saturday, Sunday or national/public holidays. There are also exchange facilities at the airport *(see page 77)*.

There is a convenient, centrally-located Thomas Cook Foreign Exchange downtown in Horton Plaza. Information line, tel: (800) 287-7362. The American Express Travel Company has a number of offices in San Diego County, including the following:

258 Broadway, tel: (619) 234-4455
7610 Hazard Center Drive,
tel: (619) 297-8101
9191 Towne Center Drive,
tel: (858) 453-0762
1020 Prospect Street, tel: (858) 459-4161
166 N El Camino Real, tel: (760) 633-1919
2131 Palomar Airport Road,
tel: (760) 431-5120.

Most offices are open Mon–Fri 9am–5.30pm and Sat 10am–4pm.

Travelers' Checks

American Express, Thomas Cook and other well-known international brands of travelers' checks are all widely used. A passport is adequate for identification, but it's a good idea to carry a driver's license or similar identification .

Credit Cards

The most commonly accepted credit cards are VISA, MasterCard, American Express, Discover and, to a lesser extent, Diners Club and JTB. The popularity of electronic banking and automatic teller machines (ATMs) makes a credit card the ideal way to organize your money for traveling. VISA, MasterCard, American Express and Discover cards are commonly accepted in ATMs.

GETTING AROUND

Trolleys

Getting there is half the fun aboard the bright red San Diego trolley, a light rail network that connects downtown San Diego with South Bay/Mexico, Old Town, Mission Valley and many East County communities. Trolleys come by every 15 minutes or so.

The Orange Line from downtown San Diego runs through the East County's Lemon Grove, La Mesa, and El Cajon to Santee.

The Blue Line from San Ysidro/Tijuana runs through Chula Vista, National City, downtown San Diego, and Old Town to Mission San Diego de Alcala in Mission Valley.

To ride the trolley you have to pre-purchase a Quick Tripper ($1–$2.25), Round Tripper ($2–$4.50), Day Tripper ($5 for unlimited travel on day of purchase) or a monthly pass ($50) at one of the trolley-stop machines. Senior citizens (60+) and the disabled get discounts. For information, tel: (619) 233-3004 or 1-(800) COMMUTE.

City Buses

San Diego operates an extensive network of Metropolitan Transit System buses. For all bus route and fare information, tel: 1-(800) COMMUTE. Bus and trolley passes can be bought at the city's Transit Store located downtown on Broadway at First Avenue.

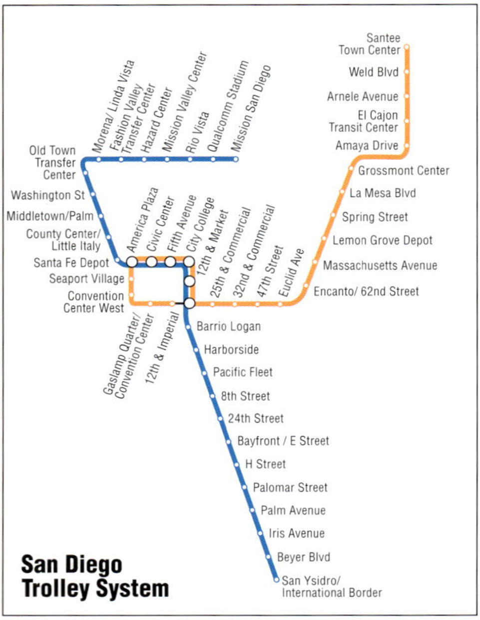

HOURS AND HOLIDAYS

Business hours

Monday–Friday 9am–5pm

Public Holidays

New Year's Day: January 1
Martin Luther King Jr's Birthday: third Monday in January
President's Day: third Monday in February
Memorial Day: last Monday in May
Independence Day: July 4
Labor Day: first Monday in September
Columbus Day: second Monday in October
Veterans Day: November 11
Thanksgiving: fourth Thursday in November
Christmas: December 25

ACCOMMODATIONS

San Diego has accommodations to suit all price ranges. The following list of selected accommodations is divided into three price categories, based on a standard double room.

$$$ = $200+
$–$$ = $100 – $200
$ = under $100

Bahia Resort Hotel
998 W Mission Bay Drive
(Mission Bay)
Tel: (858) 488-0551 or (800) 576-4229.
This beachfront resort has 321 rooms, water sports, pool, children's activities and moonlight cruises on the *Bahia Belle*. **$$**

Balboa Park Inn
3402 Park Boulevard
(Hillcrest)
Tel: (619) 298-0823 or (800) 938-8181.
Balboa Park Inn features 26 imaginative,

individually-themed suites (some of which feature fireplaces and Jacuzzis) and benefits from its close proximity to Balboa Park and the San Diego Zoo. **$–$$**

Best Western Bayside Inn
555 W Ash Street
(Downtown)
Tel: (619) 233-7500 or (800) 962-9665.
Well located in the heart of the downtown area, near San Diego Bay. Has 122 rooms, a swimming pool. **$$**

Best Western Seven Seas Lodge
411 Hotel Circle S
(Mission Valley)
Tel: (619) 291-1300 or (800) 328-1618.
307 rooms, a café, heated pool, and two spas. Good location for shopping district. **$–$$**

The Bristol
1055 First Avenue
(Downtown)
Tel: (619) 232-6141 or (800) 662-4477.
European-style, 102-room hotel with health spa and free continental breakfast. Within walking distance of the Gaslamp Quarter. **$$**

Catamaran Resort Hotel
3999 Mission Boulevard
(Mission Beach)
Tel: (858) 488-1081 or (800) 422-8386.
Beachfront resort with 313 rooms, fitness room, water sports, live entertainment and moonlight cruises on Mission Bay. **$$**

Clarion Hotel Bay View
660 K Street
(Gaslamp Quarter)
Tel: (619) 696-0234 or (800) 766-0234.
Has a health club, spa and a sundeck overlooking downtown and San Diego Bay. **$$**

Comfort Inn-Downtown
719 Ash Street
Tel: (619) 232-2525 or (800) 404-6835.
Offers 67 rooms, complimentary continental breakfast and 24-hour airport/ AMTRAK/ Greyhound shuttle. **$**

Comfort Inn and Suites Zoo/SeaWorld Area
2485 Hotel Circle Place
(Mission Valley)
Tel: (619) 881-6200 or (800) 824-0950; (in CA [800] 647-1903).
200 rooms/suites, heated pool, spa, fitness room and arcade. **$–$$**

Days Inn-Hotel Circle by SeaWorld
543 Hotel Circle S
(Mission Valley)
Tel: (619) 297-8800 or (888) 357-3959.
Featuring 280 rooms and a pool, this is a well located hotel just minutes from the zoo, SeaWorld, and beaches. **$$**

Doubletree Hotel San Diego, Mission Valley
7450 Hazard Center Drive
Tel: (619) 297-5466 or (800) 547-8010.
300 rooms, pool, health club, tennis, dining, numerous attractions, and a trolley stop. **$$**

Courtyard by Marriott
530 Broadway
(near Gaslamp Quarter)
Tel: (619) 446-3000.
Set in a magnificent 1920s marble building that used to house a bank. The Courtyard by Marriott has 245 rooms, restaurant, health club, and meeting rooms in the basement's former bank vaults. **$$**

Above: Best Western Bayside Inn

Days Inn Downtown/Zoo/ Convention Center
1449 Ninth Avenue
Tel: (619) 239-9113 or (800) DAYS-INN.
45 rooms, continental breakfast, pool. **$–$$**

Days Inn-Harbor View
1919 Pacific Highway
(Downtown)
Tel: (619) 232-1077 or (800) 822-2820.
66 rooms, continental breakfast, heated pool and free transportation to and from airport and Santa Fe Depot. **$**

El Rancho Motel
370 Orange Avenue
Coronado
Tel: 619) 435-2251.
Near North Island Naval Station. Six rooms overlook a flower-filled patio garden. **$**

Embassy Suites-San Diego Bay
601 Pacific Highway
Tel: (619) 239-2400 or (800) EMBASSY (362-2779).
Complementary breakfast and manager's reception, exercise room, pool, sauna, and spectacular bay views. 337 rooms. **$$**

Four Seasons Resort Aviara
7100 Four Seasons Point Drive
Carlsbad
Tel: (760) 603-6800.
One of North County's most splendid and tranquil getaways, the Four Seasons Resort Aviara has 331 rooms. Overlooks the Pacific, and has a golf course, tennis club and spa, a pool, and five restaurants. Nature walks along Batiquitos Lagoon. **$$$**

Glorietta Bay Inn
1630 Glorietta Boulevard
Coronado
Tel: (619) 435-3101 or (800) 283-9383.
Located in a beautiful bayside mansion that was once the home of sugar king John D Spreckels. The Glorietta Bay Inn has 89 rooms, a pool, and serves lavish continental breakfasts. **$$–$$$**

Hanalei Hotel
2270 Hotel Circle N
(Mission Valley)
Tel: (619) 297-1101 or (800) 882-0858.
The Hanalei is a tropical paradise located in Mission Valley, with 416 rooms, pool, and two restaurants. **$$**

Handlery Hotel and Resort
950 Hotel Circle N.
(Mission Valley)
Tel: (619) 298-0511 or (800) 676-6567.
Centrally located with nearby shopping and attractions. Swimming pool and adjacent golf course. **$$**

Heritage Park Bed and Breakfast Inn
2470 Heritage Park Row
(Old Town)
Tel: (619) 299-6832 or (800) 995-2470.
Characterful, 10-room Victorian mansion with feather beds, candlelit breakfasts, and afternoon teas, and the nightly screening of movie classics. **$$**

Hilton San Diego/Del Mar
15575 Jimmy Durante Boulevard
Del Mar
Tel: (858) 792-5200 or (800) HILTONS.
Adjoins Del Mar racetrack and fairgrounds, with 245 rooms, a driving range, mini-golf, and pool. **$$**

Hilton San Diego Mission Valley
901 Camino Del Rio S.
San Diego
(619) 543-9000 or (800) 733-2332.
Minutes away from area shopping, tourist attractions and Qualcomm Stadium. The Hilton San Diego Mission Valley has 350 rooms and a pool. **$$–$$$**

Hilton San Diego Resort
1775 E. Mission Bay Drive
(Mission Bay)
Tel: (619) 276-4010 or (800) HILTONS.
Bayfront resort with 357 rooms, Jacuzzi, swimming pool, fitness center, tennis courts, boat rentals, and stores. **$$–$$$**

Right: the Hotel de Coronado provides a resplendent backdrop to the beach

Holiday Inn Harbor View
1617 First Avenue
(Downtown)
Tel: (619) 239-9600 or (800) 366-3164.
Features a swimming pool, complementary transportation to and from the airport, San Diego Zoo and SeaWorld, and 218 harbor- and city-view rooms. **$$**

Holiday Inn Mission Valley Stadium
3805 Murphy Canyon Road
Tel: (858) 277-1199 or (800) 666-6996.
Pool, 174 rooms, by Qualcomm Stadium. **$**

Holiday Inn on the Bay
1355 N Harbor Drive
(Downtown)
Tel: (619) 232-3861 or (800) HOLIDAY.
600 rooms on the Embarcadero, near harbor cruises and the historic ships. Pool. **$**

Holiday Inn Select San Diego
595 Hotel Circle S.
(Mission Valley)
Tel: (619) 291-5720 or (800) 433-2131.
Features 317 rooms and a swimming pool, and is well placed for golf, shopping, and the trolley. **$–$$**

The Horton Grand
311 Island Avenue
(Gaslamp Quarter)
Tel: (619) 544-1886 or (800) 542-1886.
Historic Victorian hotel in the Gaslamp Quarter with 132 antique-filled rooms. Also has an old-fashioned restaurant. **$$**

Hotel del Coronado
1500 Orange Avenue
Coronado
Tel: (619) 522-8000 or (800) HOTEL-DEL.
A famous Victorian beauty and landmark with 692 rooms, a pool, tennis courts, fine dining, a museum, shopping promenade, and lovely white sand beaches. **$$$**

Hotel Parisi
1111 Prospect Street
La Jolla
Tel: (858) 454-1511 or (877) 4-PARISI.
This modern 20-suite, boutique-style hotel hideaway in the village of La Jolla is near shopping, dining, and La Jolla Cove. **$$$**

Howard Johnson Hotel Circle
1631 Hotel Circle S
(Mission Valley)
Tel: 619) 293-7792 or (800) 876-8937.
81 rooms, pool, free continental breakfast. **$**

Humphrey's Half Moon Inn and Suites
2303 Shelter Island Drive
Tel: (619) 224-3411 or (800) 345-9995.
Tropical setting on San Diego Bay with 182 rooms, a pool, spa, restaurant, and lounge with entertainment. **$$**

Hyatt Islandia
1441 Quivira Road
(Mission Bay)
Tel: (619) 224-1234 or (800) 233-1234.
Near SeaWorld; 422 rooms with waterfront views and swimming pool. **$$–$$$**

Hyatt Regency San Diego
1 Market Place
(Downtown)
Tel: or (800) 233-1234.
Strikingly modern hotel towering over the harbor, adjoining Seaport Village, with all 875 rooms offering bay views. Tennis, pool, health club, spa, and conference rooms. **$$$**

The Kings Inn
1333 Hotel Circle S
(Mission Valley)
Tel: (619) 297-2231 or (800) 78-KINGS.
Pool, restaurants, and140 English country-style rooms. Perfect family atmosphere. **$$**

L'Auberge Del Mar Resort and Spa
1540 Camino Del Mar
Del Mar
Tel: (858) 259-1515 or (800) 553-1336.
A 120-room luxury resort in the village of Del Mar, one block from the ocean. Has a full European spa. **$$$**

La Costa Resort and Spa
2100 Costa Del Mar Road
Carlsbad
Tel: (760) 438-9111 or (800) 854-5000.
This gigantic, 400-acre (160-ha) haven of luxury has 479 rooms, two 18-hole golf courses, 21 tennis courts, seven restaurants and lounges, and a swimming pool. La Costa Resort's world-renowned spa is the largest in the country. **$$$**

La Jolla Beach & Tennis Club
2000 Spindrift Drive
La Jolla
Tel: (858) 454-7126 or (800) 624-2582.
Well located on La Jolla Shores beach, this luxurious 90-room resort has offers 14 tennis courts, a golf course, and also a swimming pool. **$$$**

La Pensione-Little Italy
606 W Date Street
Tel: (619) 236-8000 or (800) 232-4683.
European-style hotel located in the heart of Little Italy. 80 rooms. **$**

La Valencia Hotel
1132 Prospect Street
La Jolla
Tel: (858) 454-0771 or (800) 451-0772.
Overlooking La Jolla Cove, this lovely 117-room historic hotel, built in 1926, is steps away from fine dining and shopping. **$$$**

Loews Coronado Bay Resort
4000 Coronado Bay Boulevard
Coronado
Tel: (619) 424-4000 or (800) 81-LOEWS.
This full-service resort and marina on San Diego Bay has 440 rooms, tennis courts, children's activities, restaurants, a health club, and pools. **$$$**

The Lodge at Torrey Pines
11480 N. Torrey Pines Road
La Jolla
Tel: (858) 453-4420 or (800) 995-4507.
A scenic golf resort overlooking the 18th green of the Torrey Pines Golf Course and the Pacific Ocean. **$$–$$$**

Park Manor Suites Hotel
525 Spruce Street
(Hillcrest)
Tel: (619) 291-0999 or (800) 874-2649; CA (800) 874-2649.
Uptown's answer to Old World charm. The rooftop sundeck and many of the hotel's 75 rooms offer sweeping views of the cityscape and Balboa Park. **$$**

Above: the Hyatt Regency hotel towers over the harbor

Quality Inn and Suites Downtown Harborview
1430 Seventh Avenue
(Downtown)
Tel: (619) 696-0911 or (800) 404-6835.
Complementary breakfast, pool, free 24-hour shuttle to and from airport/AMTRAK, and free local phone calls. 136 rooms. **$–$$**

Radisson Hotel Harbor View
1646 Front Street
(Downtown)
Tel: (619) 239-6800 or (800) 333-3333.
Renovated 1930s Art Deco-style hotel with 333 rooms with balconies, some with bay views, and a pool. Minutes from the airport, shopping, and nightlife. **$**

Radisson Hotel San Diego
1433 Camino Del Rio S
(Mission Valley)
Tel: (619) 260-0111 or (800) 333-3333.
The Radisson has 260 rooms, pool, spa, lounge, and fitness center. **$$**

Ramada Inn and Suites
830 Sixth Avenue
(Gaslamp Quarter)
Tel: (619) 531-8877 or (800) 664-4400.
Service and hospitality of a bygone era live on in this classic 19th-century St James Hotel building. Set in the heart of the Gaslamp Quarter, the hotel has 99 renovated rooms. Free continental breakfast. **$$**

Ramada Limited and Suites
641 Camino Del Rio S.
(Mission Valley)
Tel: (619) 295-6886 or (800) 624-1257.
Pool, spa, lounge, fitness center, and free continental breakfast. 170 rooms. Good proximity to shopping centers. **$$**

Ramada Plaza Hotel Circle
2151 Hotel Circle S.
(Mission Valley)
Tel: (619) 291-6500 or (800) 405-9102.
The pool and fitness center are the main attractions of this 182-room hotel. **$$**

Rancho Bernardo Inn
17550 Bernardo Oaks Drive
(Rancho Bernardo)
Tel: (858) 675-8500.
Prize-winning inland hotel with tennis, pool, spa, championship golf. 287 rooms. **$$–$$$**

The Regency Plaza Hotel
1515 Hotel Circle S
(Mission Valley)
Tel: (619) 881-6900 or (800) 489-9210.
Many of the 217 rooms have balconies and views of the valley. Pool, spa, sundeck, restaurant, lounge, and fitness room. **$$$**

Rodeway Inn-Zoo/Downtown/Convention Center
833 Ash Street
(Downtown)
Tel: (619) 239-2285 or (800) 522-1528.
45 rooms and free breakfast. Near Balboa Park and San Diego Zoo. **$**

San Diego Marriott Hotel and Marina
333 W Harbor Drive
Tel: (619) 234-1500 or (800) 228-9290.
Double-towered landmark on San Diego's bayfront with 1,355 rooms. The pool is a tropical oasis next to a yacht club and marina. Excellent for lounges, restaurants, and conference facilities. Next to a convention center. **$$–$$$**

San Diego Marriott Mission Valley
8750 Rio San Diego Drive
Tel: (619) 692-3800.
350 rooms with balconies, heated pool, whirlpool, exercise room, and tennis court. Near area shopping. **$$**

San Diego Paradise Point Resort
1404 W Vacation Road
(Mission Bay)
Tel: (858) 274-4630 or (800) 344-2626.
An expansive, all-inclusive bayfront resort with 462 rooms, putting course, fitness center, six pools, sauna, whirlpool, marina, masseuse, botanical tours, cycle rentals, and jogging course. **$$–$$$**

Sheraton Harbor Island
1380 Harbor Island Drive
(Downtown)
Tel: (619) 692-2300
Bayfront hotel with 699 rooms, pool, health club and spa, tennis courts, and marina cruises. **$$–$$$**

Sommerset Suite Hotel
606 Washington Street
(Hillcrest)
Tel: (619) 692-5200 or (800) 962-9665.
80 suites in the heart of Hillcrest (near shopping and dining), pool and free breakfast. **$**

Club Sunterra Harbour Lights Resort
911 Fifth Avenue
(Gaslamp Quarter)
Tel: (619) 233-3300
The Gaslamp's polished new Art Deco-inspired property has one and two-bedroom suites with partial kitchen. **$$**

Town and Country Resort and Convention Center
500 Hotel Circle N
(Mission Valley)
Tel: (619) 291-7131 or (800) 772-8527.
A Mission Valley landmark with 966 rooms, a beautiful garden setting, four swimming pools, Jacuzzi, spa/health club, golf, and five restaurants. Near Fashion Valley Center and the trolley. **$$$**

U S Grant Hotel
326 Broadway
Tel: (619) 232-3121 or
CA (800) 334-6957 or (800) 237-5029.
This historic hotel was built by President Grant's son in 1910, and it resembles a grand English estate with its glittery chandeliers, marble floors, hardwood paneling, and a beautiful dining room. Across the street from Horton Plaza. **$$$**

Welk Resort Center
8860 Lawrence Welk Drive
Escondido
Tel: (760) 749-3000 or (800) 932-9355.
Tucked away in the hills of North County, this rural resort created by Lawrence Welk has 137 rooms, 286 villa-style condos, two 18-hole golf courses, a Broadway-style theater, shopping plaza, restaurants, and an entertaining museum. **$$–$$$**

The Westgate Hotel
1055 Second Avenue
(Downtown)
Tel: (619) 238-1818 or (800) 221-3802.
This European-style hotel, a local landmark in elegance, has 223 rooms and is centrally located near the theater, civic center, and Gaslamp Quarter. **$$$**

The Westin Horton Plaza
910 Broadway Circle
(Downtown)
Tel: (619) 239-2200 or (800)-6-WESTIN.
As colorful and inviting as its Horton Plaza neighbor, the Westin has 450 rooms, two restaurants, lounges, a health club, and a swimming pool. **$$–$$$**

Emerald Plaza Hotel
400 W Broadway
(Downtown)
Tel: (619) 239-4500.
436 rooms, a restaurant, lounge, health club, and a pool. Recognizable by its Emerald City-like, green, neon-topped towers. Near the Santa Fe Depot. **$$$**

Budget Accomodations

San Diego Hotel Reservations
Tel: (858) 627-9300 or (800)-SAVE-CASH.
Free hotel reservation service with lots of discounted and unpublished rates at more than 200 San Diego hotels.

There follows a list of budget (up to $50 for a standard double room) accommodations.

Campus Hitching Post Motel
6235 El Cajon Boulevard
Tel: (619) 583-1456.
Just 30 rooms situated near San Diego State University.

Days Inn-Mission Bay by SeaWorld
2575 Clairemont Drive
Tel: (619) 275-5700 or (800) 457-8080.
100-room establishment just one block from Mission Bay, featuring complementary continental breakfast and coffee.

Embassy Hotel
3645 Park Boulevard
Tel: (619) 296-3141.
80 rooms in residential neighborhood.

Good Nite Inn
4545 Waring Road
(Mission Valley)
Tel: (619) 286-7000 or (800) 648-3466.
93 rooms, swimming pool.

Hostelling International-Point Loma
3790 Udall Street
Tel: 619) 223-4778 or (800) 909-4776 (hostel code 44).
Dormitory rooms 1 mile from the beach.

Hostelling International-San Diego
521 Market Sreet
Tel: (619) 525-1531 or (800) 909-4776 (hostel code 43).
Dormitory-style accommodations.

J Street Inn
222 J Street
(Gaslamp Quarter)
Tel: (619) 696-6922.
J Street Inn's 221 rooms with kitchenettes benefit from a simple and modern design. Near trolley and convention center.

Ocean Beach International Backpackers Hostel
4961 Newport Avenue
Tel: (619) 223-SURF (7873) or (800) 339-7263.
Hostel solely for international travelers. Free airport, train, and bus pickup.

Ramada Limited-SeaWorld
3747 Midway Drive
Tel: (619) 225-1295 or (800) 652-2355.
One mile (1.6km) from SeaWorld and adjacent to shopping. Free breakfast.

Sleepy Time Motel
4545 Mission Bay Drive
(Mission Bay)
Tel: (858) 483-4222.
The 66 rooms are within walking distance of Mission Bay.

Super 8 Motel
4380 Alvarado Canyon Road
(Mission Valley)
Tel: (619) 281-2222 or (800) 828-8111.
This Super 8 has just over 100 rooms, and guests receive a complementary breakfast.

Trade Winds Motel
4305 Mission Bay Drive
(Mission Bay)
Tel: (858) 273-4616.
The Trade Winds's 18 rooms are two blocks from beaches and just across the street from Mission Bay golf course.

USA Hostels-San Diego
726 Fifth Avenue
Tel: (619) 232-3100 or (800) 438-8622.
International hostel catering to travelers on long-term expeditions.

Vagabond Inn
625 Hotel Circle S
(Mission Valley)
Tel: (619) 297-1691 or (800) 522-1555.
Don't be put off by the name: there's a pool, Jacuzzi, and complementary continental breakfast.

Above: bed & breakfast

EMERGENCIES

Doctors here have modern equipment and facilities but health coverage in the US can be expensive, so take out a comprehensive health-insurance policy before traveling.

Medical Services for Travelers

After-Hours Emergency Dentistry
945 Hornblend Street, A
Tel: (619) 586-1207.
Nights, Saturday, Sunday, holidays.

Travelmed, Inc
Tel: (800) 878-3627.
Doctors, dentists, chiropractors, nurses, 24 hours, 7 days. Hotel calls and office visits.

Hospitals

Children's Hospital
3020 Children's Way
Tel: (858) 576-1700.

Scripps Mercy Hospital
4077 Fifth Avenue
(Hillcrest)
Tel: (619) 294-8111.

Sharp Memorial Hospital
7901 Frost Street
Tel: (858) 541-3400.

UCSD Medical Center
200 W Arbor Drive
(Hillcrest)
Tel: (619) 543-6222.

24-hour Emergency Numbers
Fire, Police and Ambulance: 911.

MAIL & TELEPHONE

Telephone

The country code for the US is 1. The area codes for San Diego are 619, 858 and 760. Local calls from public phones cost 35 cents for the first 3 minutes. You don't need to dial the three-digit area code when calling from within the same code. When calling a number outside the area code you're in, dial 1, then the area code and number. Numbers beginning with 800, 888 or 877 are toll-free.

Some pay phones use pre-paid cards, available from post offices, newsstands, grocery and convenience stores. They come in denominations of $5 and up, and can be used to make any calls.

Calling Overseas

International calls can be made directly from most phones – dial 011, then the country code, city area code and then the local number. For operator assistance, dial 0.

Postal Services

Post Offices are open Mon–Fri 9am–5pm and Sat 9am–noon. There is no mail delivery on Sun or national holidays. The main post office will hold visitors' mail for 30 days (address: c/o General Delivery, San Diego Main Post Office, San Diego, CA 92130).

USEFUL INFORMATION

Geography

San Diego County stretches over 760 sq miles (1,968 sq km) of scenic topography – beaches, lagoons, canyons, foothills, deserts, and mountains. Its greatest east–west length is 80 miles (129km); north to south it reaches 70 miles (113km). It's bounded by the Mexico border to the south, by the expansive Camp Pendleton US Marine base and the evergreen mountains of Cleveland National Forest to the north (a natural buffer between San Diego and Orange and Riverside counties). The Pacific Ocean hugs the county's western side and the stark, beautiful, desolate deserts of Imperial County border its eastern edge.

Population

San Diego is the seventh largest city in the US with a population of approximately 1.2 million. The current population of San Diego County is estimated to be 2.8 million.

USEFUL ADDRESSES

Balboa Park Visitors Center
1549 El Prado (House of Hospitality) (Balboa Park)
Tel: (619) 239-0512.
Information on exhibits and activities in the park, and elsewhere. Open daily 9am–4pm.

Downtown Information Center
225 Broadway
(Downtown)
Tel: (619) 235-2222.
Information on downtown neighborhoods.

International Visitors Center
11 Horton Plaza (Downtown)
Tel: (619) 236-1212
sdinfo@sandiego.org
www.sandiego.org
Has a multilingual staff.

San Diego East Visitors Bureau
4695 Nebo Drive (La Mesa Railroad Museum) La Mesa
Tel: (619) 463-1166.
Information about San Diego's East County sights, attractions, and museums.

San Diego North Convention and Visitors Bureau
720 N Broadway, Escondido
Tel: (760) 745-4741 or (800) 848-3336.
Information on San Diego's North County beaches and back country, golf courses, wineries, outdoor recreation, and attractions.

San Diego Visitor Information Center
2688 E Mission Bay Drive (Mission Bay)
Tel: (619) 276-8200.
Information, discounted accommodations, and tickets to attractions. Free maps and restaurant guides. Open daily.

Travelers Aid Society
306 Walnut Street, 21 (Downtown)
Tel: (619) 295-8393.
Information on San Diego attractions, accommodations, and emergency travel assistance. At Lindbergh Field, the Broadway Pier (at B Street) and Santa Fe Depot.

FURTHER READING

Insight Guide: California, Apa Publications 1999. Lavishly photographed and fully revised, with detailed information on sights.
The Explorers by Richard F Pourade (Union Tribune, 1960)
California of the South: A History by John Steven McGroarty (S J Clarke, 1933)
Where California Began by Winifred Davidson (McIntyre, 1929)
Rails of the Silver Gate: the Spreckels San Diego Empire by Richard V Dodge (Canadian Pacific Railroad Journal, 1960)
Five California Architects by Esther McCoy (Reinhold, 1960)
Inventing Wyatt Earp by Allen Barra (Carroll and Graf, 1998)
Scripps: The Divided Dynasty by Jack Casserly (Donald I Fine, 1993)
Ellen Browning Scripps, journalist and idealist by Albert Britt (OUP 1961)
The Story of New San Diego and its Founder by Elizabeth C MacPhail (Pioneer, 1969)
Julian City by Charles P LeMenager (Eagle Rock Publ, Ramona, 1992)
Discover San Diego by Leander and Rosalie Peik (Peik's Enterprises, San Diego, 1992)

Right: keeping the streets safe

ACKNOWLEDGEMENTS

All photography	**Jerry Dennis** *except*
42b	**Museum of Contemporary Art, San Diego**
59	**San Diego Convention and Visitors Bureau/Gene Warneke**
13b	**Thomas Gilcrease Institute of American History and Art, Oklahoma**
16	**Topham Picture Point**
12	**Vautier de-Nanxe**

Cartography **Berndtson & Berndtson**

© APA Publications GmbH & Co. Verlag KG Singapore Branch, Singapore

Left: sun and surf north of Del Mar

The travel guides that replace a tour guide – now better than ever with more listings and a fresh new design

INSIGHT Pocket Guides

Insight Pocket Guides pioneered a new approach to guidebooks, introducing the concept of the authors as "local hosts" who would provide readers with personal recommendations, just as they would give honest advice to a friend who came to stay. They also included a full-size pull-out map. Now, to cope with the needs of the 21st century, new editions in this growing series are being given a new look to make them more practical to use, and restaurant and hotel listings have been greatly expanded.

INSIGHT GUIDES

The world's largest collection of visual travel guides

Now in association with

Discovery CHANNEL

Also from Insight Guides...

Insight Guides is the classic series, providing the complete picture with expert and informative text and stunning photography. Each book is an ideal travel planner, a reliable on-the-spot companion – and a superb visual souvenir of a trip. 193 titles.

Insight Maps are designed to complement the guidebooks. They provide full mapping of major destinations, and their laminated finish gives them ease of use and durability. 100 titles.

Insight Compact Guides are handy reference books, modestly priced yet comprehensive. The text, pictures and maps are all cross-referenced, making them ideal books to consult while seeing the sights. 127 titles.

INSIGHT POCKET GUIDE TITLES

Aegean Islands
Algarve
Alsace
Amsterdam
Athens
Atlanta
Bahamas
Baja Peninsula
Bali
Bali Bird Walks
Bangkok
Barbados
Barcelona
Bavaria
Beijing
Berlin
Bermuda
Bhutan
Boston
Brisbane & the Gold Coast
British Columbia
Brittany
Brussels
Budapest
California, Northern
Canton
Cape Town
Chiang Mai
Chicago
Corfu
Corsica
Costa Blanca
Costa Brava
Costa del Sol
Costa Rica
Crete
Croatia
Denmark
Dubai
Fiji Islands
Florence
Florida
Florida Keys
French Riviera (Côte d'Azur)
Gran Canaria
Hawaii
Hong Kong
Hungary
Ibiza
Ireland
Ireland's Southwest
Israel
Istanbul
Jakarta
Jamaica
Kathmandu Bikes & Hikes
Kenya
Kraków
Kuala Lumpur
Lisbon
Loire Valley
London
Los Angeles
Macau
Madrid
Malacca
Maldives
Mallorca
Malta
Manila
Melbourne
Mexico City
Miami
Montreal
Morocco
Moscow
Munich
Nepal
New Delhi
New Orleans
New York City
New Zealand
Oslo and Bergen
Paris
Penang
Perth
Phuket
Prague
Provence
Puerto Rico
Quebec
Rhodes
Rome
Sabah
St. Petersburg
San Diego
San Francisco
Sarawak
Sardinia
Scotland
Seville, Cordoba & Granada
Seychelles
Sicily
Sikkim
Singapore
Southeast England
Southern Spain
Sri Lanka
Stockholm
Switzerland
Sydney
Tenerife
Thailand
Tibet
Toronto
Tunisia
Turkish Coast
Tuscany
Venice
Vienna
Vietnam
Yogjakarta
Yucatán Peninsula

INDEX